MW01593582

# SEEKING

## *JESUS*

### FINDING LIFE
### IN THE
### MEANS OF GRACE

## TIMOTHY C. TENNENT

 Seedbed

Scripture quotations, unless otherwise indicated, are taken from The Holy Bible, English Standard Version®, ESV®, copyright © 2001 by Crossway Bibles, a division of Good News Publishers. Used by permission. All rights reserved.

Scripture quotations marked NIV are taken from the Holy Bible, New International Version®, NIV® Copyright © 1973, 1978, 1984, 2011 by Biblica, Inc.™ Used by permission of Zondervan. All rights reserved worldwide. www.zondervan.com. The "NIV" and "New International Version" are trademarks registered in the United States Patent and Trademark Office by Biblica, Inc.™ All rights reserved worldwide.

Scripture quotations marked RSV are taken from the Revised Standard Version of the Bible, copyright © 1946, 1952, and 1971 National Council of the Churches of Christ in the United States of America. Used by permission. All rights reserved.

Scripture quotations marked KJV are taken from the Holy Bible, King James Version, Cambridge, 1796.

Printed in the United States of America

*Cover design by Strange Last Name*
*Page design and layout by PerfecType, Nashville, Tennessee*

**Tennent, Timothy C.**
 Seeking Jesus : finding life in the means of grace / Timothy C. Tennent. – Franklin, Tennessee : Seedbed Publishing, ©2021.

 pages ; cm .

 ISBN 9781628249170 (hardcover)
 ISBN 9781628249187 (paperback)
 ISBN 9781628249194 (Mobi)
 ISBN 9781628249200 (ePub)
 ISBN 9781628249217 (uPDF)
 OCLC 1263024276

 1. Grace (Theology). 2. Sacraments. 3. Spiritual life—Christianity.
 4. Spiritual exercises. I. Title.

BT761.T46 2021                234.12           2021944685

SEEDBED PUBLISHING
Franklin, Tennessee
seedbed.com

To Mark and Jackie Royster,
whose Spirit-filled lives have been a
means of grace to many

# Contents

# Christ the Fountainhead of the Means of Grace

Scripture Background: Colossians 1:15–23

A number of years ago Willow Creek performed a survey of two thousand churches and more than a half million believers to find out what helped people grow spiritually. The assumption that has driven most churches is that any church activity will result in spiritual growth—just get people involved. Many churches have groups ranging from fellowship groups, to prayer groups, to groups that help people with their finances, or raising children, or losing weight. What they found was that only two groups among dozens that churches invest in actually helped people grow spiritually. Those were groups that focused on prayer and on Bible study. What is remarkable is that without real-izing it, Willow Creek stumbled upon two of the means of grace through a survey. If they had just read Wesley's sermon on the means of grace (sermon #16), they could have saved the three million dollars they invested in these church surveys.

The idea of the "means of grace" refers to divinely instituted means by which we can grow spiritually and includes all the ways God uses to extend His grace into our lives so that we become more like Him. Another way of putting this is that the means of grace conform us to the image of Jesus Christ—the goal of the Christian life. The concept is rooted in Scripture, though the phrase "means of grace" arises in later Christian tradition. It is taught in question #68 of the 1563 *Heidelberg Catechism* and in question #154 of the 1647 *Westminster Catechism*. Indeed, the phrase "means of grace" has a long history in both Roman Catholic and Puritan theology. But in the eighteenth century, John Wesley made it central to the process of sanctification among the people called Methodists. Prayer and reading God's Word lead Wesley's list, among others like fasting and taking the Eucharist, serving the poor, and so forth.

We will explore many of the means of grace in this book, but it is vital to point out as a foundational truth that Jesus Christ is the fountainhead of all the means of grace. In the opening pages of his sermon "The Means of Grace," Wesley warns us all not to confuse the *means* of grace with either the *source* or the *end* of grace. The means separated from the end is "less than nothing and vanity." In fact, Wesley says that doing a lot of religious activity in and of itself is to turn "God's arms against himself; of keeping Christianity out of the heart by those very means which were ordained for the bringing it in." In other words, there is no inherent power—like some kind of magic—in the means of grace, even though God ordained them, because we cannot confuse the means for the end. There are many means of grace, but only one end of grace; namely, Christ Himself. And there is only one source of grace—the triune God, though our focus here will be upon Christ as the central means of grace. So, the means of grace do not begin with what we do but who He is, lest we get off on the wrong track at the outset. This is why our text for this chapter is Colossians 1:15–23 and the following section is called *The Preeminence of Jesus Christ*. In practicing the means of grace, we are to be *seeking Jesus*.

# The Preeminence of Jesus Christ Colossians 1:15–20 (Christ Hymn) and 21–23 (Admonition)

The passage found in Colossians 1:15–20 is likely an early creedal hymn about Christ that Paul inserts into this part of his letter. There are quite a few of these creedal hymns in the New Testament (including Luke 1:47–55; 68–79; 2:29–32; Heb. 1:5–12; Eph. 5:14; 2 Tim. 2:11–13; and Rev. 4:8, 11; 5:9–10, 12–13). So, we have right in the New Testament a glimpse of very early Christology from the earliest hymns of the church. Isn't it wonderful how the early church would embed doctrine and theology together in an act of worship? This hymn (vv. 15–20) celebrates Christ's supremacy over creation and redemption. We become sharers in His preeminence and glory because we are "in Christ." The last few verses, 21–23, are the *application* of the hymn to our lives, and this is precisely how I will use this early hymn in this chapter.

There are many suggestions about the background of this hymn, but I think the most convincing explanation is that this is a Christological hymn written in light of the creation account in Genesis 1 and 2. In other words, it is the creation account from Genesis set as an act of worship that puts Christ at the center of both creation and redemption. The hymn makes five central affirmations about Christ and one grand proclamation to undergird all the others.

1. Christ is the image of the invisible God—v. 15
2. Christ is the firstborn over all creation—v. 15
3. Christ is the creator and sustainer of all things—vv. 16–17
4. Christ is the head of the church—v. 18
5. Christ is the reconciler of all things—v. 20

Because He is the Lord of both creation (vv. 15–17) and redemption (vv. 18, 20), we have woven in with these five the summative statement of them all in verse 19, which declares that "in him all the fullness of God was pleased to dwell." This full-throated declaration of the deity of Christ is repeated in Colossians 2:9, so I don't see this as just another declaration in the list but the very foundation that makes the other five possible. Jesus Christ is God in the flesh.

This passage (with these central five affirmations plus the grand proclamation) forms one of the most important bedrock Christological passages in the New Testament. This hymn was crucial in the discussions leading up to the formal understanding of who Christ is by the early church. In this chapter I will focus on the first, second, and fifth of these.

## *Christ Is the Image of the Invisible God—v. 15*

Christ has made the invisible God fully visible and manifest. The apostle John makes this point in his gospel when he declares that "no one has ever seen God; the only God, who is at the Father's side, he has made him known" (John 1:18). This hymn takes it a step further by declaring that Jesus is the perfect image or reflection of God. The doctrine of the image of God is foundational to the creation account: "Let us make man in our image, after our likeness . . . So God created man in his own image, in the image of God he created him; male and female, he created them" (Gen. 1:26–27). The phrase "image of God" is applied to no other creative act of God other than the creation of man and woman. This separates us from the rest of creation. We represent God's imprint, His presence in the world. To be created in the image of God means, among other things, that we have been called to be coregents with God in extending (via our faithful stewardship and dominion) His rule and reign into the world. But, as image-bearers we have marred that image and exchanged our dominion role for one that places us in bondage to sin. The phrase "image of God" is never mentioned in the Old Testament after Genesis 9:6. Now, in Christ, the image of God has been fully restored and made manifest in Christ who reflects the image of God in a singular way. Because Christ is fully God *and* fully man, He not only reflects God's revelation of Himself to us but also shows us what we are destined to be as image-bearers. Jesus is the revelation of both God and man to us!

This is the crucial bridge upon which all the means of grace are focused to conform you and me as image-bearers (marred by sin) into the full image of Christ (free from the bondage of sin). Therefore, the means of grace have been given to us to fully restore the image of God in us. The means of grace are God's great mirror repair job!

The image of God explodes afresh in the New Testament, but it is now focused on Christ as the image of God. It is not just here in Colossians 1:15 but also in 2 Corinthians 4:4 and Romans 8:29. From the recommissioning of Noah until the coming of Christ, the image of God is portrayed through a kind of anti-image, where we are not regarded as image-bearers but as idol-bearers. The Old Testament is filled with the phrases "false image," "graven image," "idolatrous image," and so forth. But doesn't a false image imply that there must be a *true* one, of which this is a departure? The image that idolatry mars is the image of God. We who were made in the image of God have turned and are fashioning false images of God, using stone, wood, metal, and eventually bank accounts or whatever else we reflect and value. All idolatry is a kind of anti-image bearing. The means of grace are designed to deliver you and me from all idolatry and fully restore the image of God in us.

Our text reminds us that Jesus Christ is the image of God in human flesh. Christ comes as a second Adam (Rom. 5:12–21), and He comes, in part, to fully restore the image of God, which has been mangled and severely damaged through idolatry. In the New Testament, the whole notion of the image of God is applied supremely to Jesus Christ, who is the ultimate visible representation of the invisible God of the universe. As the fullness of deity, Jesus perfectly images God in all His fullness, but as the fullness of humanity, Jesus perfectly shows us what it means to bear God's image in our redeemed humanity. The New Testament teaches that Jesus in both His deity and His full humanity manifests the true, unbroken image of God because the two natures of Christ—His humanity and His deity—are united in the one person. You cannot separate them. God has stepped into this world. We call this the incarnation. G. K. Chesterton once famously said that even those who reject the doctrine of the incarnation are different for having heard of it. It is in Christ that the entire broken world is refashioned and, once again, restored to reflect God's image. As the perfect image of God, Jesus Christ completes the original vocation of humanity and thereby shows us who we were originally intended to be. Christ is God's image in the world, fully active, fully alive, in a way we have not seen since the dawn of creation. The means of grace are given to conform us back to that unmarred image seen in the restored humanity of Christ as the second Adam.

## *Christ Is the Firstborn over All Creation—v. 15*

This phrase has caused great confusion in the church, because calling Christ the "firstborn" seems, on a superficial reading, to undermine traditional, orthodox Christology that affirms the preexistence of Christ from all eternity (Heb. 1:6; Rev. 1:5). What does it mean to affirm that He is the "firstborn over all creation"? The term *firstborn* is used in a way it would be understood by a Jew in the first century. The term appears 130 times in the Greek version of the Old Testament known as the Septuagint. A survey of those 130 times reveals that there are two ways it is used. The first, obvious way, is a *biological* firstborn child who is born and is temporally prior to other children who are born in a family. But the second way is a *declared* title, a manifest position that has nothing to do with biology. For example, in Psalm 89:27 God says of David, "I will make him the firstborn" (i.e., David is granted an exalted position and a greater inheritance symbolized by firstborn even though he is not God's biological offspring at all, nor the biological firstborn of his own family, having seven older brothers). Thus, one could be "appointed" or "declared" a firstborn as a title or position.

The phrase "firstborn over all creation" has three dimensions to it. First, it refers to the special prerogative given to the eternally begotten Son. As the firstborn son he is granted an inheritance, one aspect of which is that he is the Lord over the creation. When the Bible uses a word like *firstborn*, it does not mean that there was a time when the Son of God did not exist. It means rather that He is granted the inheritance of the whole creation, including all the nations, as the eternal Son of God and is therefore eternally begotten.

Second, the word *firstborn* is also shorthand for the doctrine of the incarnation, and this *does* have a temporal aspect to it. As the incarnate one, He did take on human flesh in real time and space, born as the God-man through the womb of Mary. God *became* a man—with no compromise in the full force of that declaration! God in Jesus Christ enters into the creation of His own making. As Adam was in a certain respect the firstborn of the first creation, Jesus Christ, as the second Adam, is the firstborn over the new creation.

Third, the phrase is also shorthand for His status as the resurrected one; He is the firstfruits of the resurrection. Jesus Christ is the first to be resurrected as we will all someday be resurrected. Therefore, Jesus is the firstborn of this new redeemed humanity. Our resurrection is all linked to His resurrection since He is the head, the firstfruits, and firstborn of the redeemed community.

Just as Christ reclaims and makes manifest what it means to be in the unblemished image of God and the means of grace are given to reconform us to the image of God, so, too, Christ being declared the "firstborn over creation" is about us reclaiming our rightful inheritance in Christ. In the Old Testament, being a firstborn son carried a special place of privilege with special claims to inheritance. In the incarnation God sends His firstborn Son, Jesus Christ—the only begotten one—to earth to reclaim His lost children and adopt us as His sons and daughters, declaring us all to have the inheritance of first-born sons because we are now in Christ. Romans 8:23 declares that we are awaiting our full adoption as sons by which we can claim our full inheritance. Hebrews 12:23 calls us "the assembly of the firstborn." If you are a woman reading these passages, it is good and right for you to celebrate that you are an elect daughter of the Most High God. But, as a woman, you are still a full inheritor of the claims of sonship, which is bound up with Christ's title as the firstborn. All women are declared inheritors of sonship, even as they are also daughters. Women are "daughtered sons." Men, also, though we are biologically sons, are full members of the bride of Christ. My being a male no more robs me of being part of the bride of Christ than being a woman robs our female readers of being part of the inheritance of sonship as part of the theology of the firstborn. It is not about biology but a declared status about our inheritance. God is beyond human gender, but He uses the relational language of fatherhood and sonship in order to communicate His redemptive purposes. If you are in Christ, you are inheritors of all the inheritance that Christ embodies and the means of grace have been given so that every one of you can claim your inheritance.

## *Christ Is the Reconciler of All Things—v. 20*

In Colossians 1:19 Paul says, "In him all the fullness of God was pleased to dwell." He repeats it in Colossians 2:9—"For in him the whole fullness of deity dwells bodily," which is the grand takeaway or central theme that makes all the others possible. The fifth and final declaration is that Christ is the reconciler of all things. Jesus is the fountainhead of cosmic reconciliation. Paul says in 1:20 that God is working "through him to reconcile to himself all things, whether on earth or in heaven, making peace by the blood of his cross." Just as there are three dimensions to Christ's title as firstborn, there are three dimensions to His work of cosmic reconciliation. First, it is an *eschatological*, or "end time" statement, pointing to the end point in human history when God will set all things right. Even those opposed to Him will eventually acknowledge His lordship in the way we see expressed in the famous passage in Philippians: "Every knee should bow . . . and every tongue confess that Jesus Christ is Lord" (2:10–11). Second, it is a truth declaration like the angels on the day of resurrection:

"He is not here, He is risen." The Colossians hymn declares a cosmic truth to the world that Jesus is the reconciler. Paul is speaking about what is, not about the myriad ways people may or may not reflect this truth.

Third, it is a long-view, aspirational, historical statement. Even in the face of the unbelieving world, Paul is anticipating the global mission of the church, which will bring the gospel to the ends of the earth. The gospel is, at heart, a message of reconciliation! All three of these dimensions celebrate the supremacy of Christ's identity as the fountainhead and sole source of God's work of reconciliation.

The means of grace are not just about what God does in your *heart*. They are also enabling you to embody reconciliation. Many of you are carrying around inside of you deep hurts, disappointments, betrayals. We all see the challenges of racism in the world. This has given birth to anxiety, anger, the inability to trust anyone, cynicism, and for some, a foreboding sense of despair. The means of grace move us toward reconciliation, with our past, our parents, all races of people, and all those with whom we have a broken relationship, and most of all, with God Himself.

Christ came into this world for you. Listen to Paul's words of application after the end of this amazing

Colossians hymn: "He has now reconciled in his body of flesh by his death, in order to present you holy and blameless and above reproach before him" (1:22). The whole universe is moving toward reconciliation. God is the victor over all the world's brokenness and all the ways we mar the image of God. The means of grace are given for that very purpose.

So, in summary,

1. Jesus Christ is the means of grace through which we become conformed, once again, to the image of God.
2. The means of grace enable us to fully claim our inheritance "in Christ" through which we are sharers in the full rights of the firstborn.
3. And the means of grace enable us to move from being alienated from God to being reconciled to God and one another.

The rest of this book will develop all the particulars of the means of grace with Christ as the fountainhead, standing as both the source and the goal of all the means of grace.

# Chapter One

# The Church as a Means of Grace

*The Universal Call and the Radical Transformation*

Scriptural Background: Ephesians 4:17–5:20

The church is itself a means of grace. The passage from Ephesians 4:17–5:20 has several headings suggested by modern editors. The NIV (1984) calls it "Living as Children of the Light." The ESV calls this section "The New Life." The RSV calls it the "The Old Life and the New." I would suggest titling this section of Paul's letter to the Ephesians (4:17–5:20) "The Transformed Life," because that is the theme of this section. Paul is addressing the church in Ephesus with a particular focus on the influx of Gentiles into the church and the need to make sure that these believers with no background in Jewish practices of holiness become partakers of holiness and embodied righteousness, as well as the necessity for the church to be a living, transformative people who vibrantly extend the sanctifying grace of God.

## The Transformed Life

Paul highlights in this section the life that is ours when we become partakers of the sanctifying grace of God. At verse 17, Paul begins boldly by bearing witness to a remarkable transformation that takes place among the people of God, the church. He is testifying to a new, radical identity that embraces, yet supersedes, all other identities.

In every culture the defining marks of identity are ethnicity, gender, language, social status, and cultural experience. These are the five leading, powerful, and formative forces that shape our identity. The gospel does not obliterate these, and even in John's vision of the future church at the end of time, he sees men and women of every tribe, tongue, and language worshiping the Lord. But, Paul is saying that our *new* identity in Christ is so powerful and so transformative that this becomes an altogether new and controlling identity that supersedes without supplanting all other identities. We belong to

Christ and we are the baptized community of those who have been united to His life. In today's identity-fractured culture, this insight alone is priceless. This is why Paul can say in Colossians 3:11 that in Christ "there is not Greek or Jew, circumcised or uncircumcised, barbarian, Scythian, slave, free; but Christ is all, and in all." Being in Christ is your new and primary identity!

Paul's testimony goes on to set forth a new life that is a stunning alternative to all the world's ways of looking at the human experience. We are no longer to walk in step with the Gentile world from which we once drew our identity. Once we were captivated by what was going on with Taylor Swift, Beyoncé, or Kevin Hart; we really cared about the latest Instagram shots or YouTube videos that went viral, the outcome of some fantasy football game, the latest clothing styles, or even our ethnic identity. But, those things fade, or are put in their proper perspective, when we draw our identity from Jesus Christ. Paul notes two trajectories of the old life in the flesh: the mind and the heart. Paul begins by saying that we are no longer to walk as the Gentiles walk in "the futility of their minds" (Eph. 4:17), which implies an emptiness, or a purposelessness, or even instability in their thinking. Second, our hearts have become corrupt. We, as humans, have given ourselves over to "sensuality, greedy to practice every kind of impurity" (v. 19). In other words, our hearts and our minds have become corrupted and cut off from the life of God. This does not imply that every unbeliever is marked by these specific traits, but that these are the kinds of qualities that get reproduced over and over in the lives of those who remain disconnected from Christ. The particularities may vary, but the corruption of the mind and the heart is the basic theme, though it may manifest itself in many different ways.

So, here's the setting: brand-new Gentile believers are coming into the church, and Paul is earnestly hoping that they can be effectively incorporated into the people of God.

This is where the church comes in as the means of grace through which God extends His transforming grace into our lives. The church is always a means of grace to the world because we offer both the grace to radically and unconditionally and universally embrace a lost world with the love of Jesus Christ *and* the grace of God that enables us to flourish and be transformed into the very likeness of Jesus Christ. These are the two ways the church expresses itself as a means of grace—through the radical call and the radical transformation.

# Radical, Open Call of the Church to the World

We all have seen signs in front of churches that try to express our open, radical love in Jesus Christ for the world. One sign that is used around the country was taken from a book entitled *A Step Along the Way*[1] and expresses this open call in a direct way:

> We extend a special welcome to those who are single, married, divorced, gay, filthy rich, dirt poor, y no hable Ingles. We extend a special welcome to those who are crying newborns, skinny as a rail, or could afford to lose a few pounds. . . . We don't care if you're . . . more Catholic than the Pope, or haven't been in church since little Joey's Baptism. We extend a special welcome to those who are over 60 but not grown up yet, and to teenagers who are growing up too fast. We welcome soccer moms, NASCAR dads, starving artists, tree-huggers, latte-sippers, vegetarians, junk-food eaters. We welcome

1. Stephen J. Pope, *A Step Along the Way: Models of Christian Service* (Maryknoll, NY: Orbis Press, 2015), 123–24. The author attributes the first appearance of this sign to the Lady of Lourdes Catholic Church in Daytona Beach, Florida.

those who are in recovery or are still addicted. We welcome you if you're having problems, or you're down in the dumps, or if you don't like "organized religion" (we've been there, too). If you blew all your offering at the dog track, you're welcome here. We offer special welcome to those who think the earth is flat, work too hard, don't work, can't spell, or came because grandma is in town and wanted to go to church. We welcome those who are inked, pierced, or both. We offer a special welcome to those who could use a prayer right now, had religion shoved down your throat as a kid, or got lost in traffic and wound up here by mistake. . . . We welcome tourists, seekers, doubters, bleeding hearts . . . and you!

Let's examine this sign and see how it fits into our passage of Scripture. This sign is a powerful expression of the prevenient grace of God. It is an expression of the "whosoever" of John 3:16. It is an expression of that powerful text in Isaiah 55:1, "Come, everyone who thirsts, come to the waters; and he who has no money, come, buy and eat!" It is this text which Jesus Himself draws on in John 7:37 when He cries out in a loud voice at the Jewish festival: "If anyone thirsts, let him come to me and drink." This is the theological point Paul is making when he says in Romans, "While we were still sinners, Christ died for us" (5:8).

In the language of our text, this sign acknowledges that we all come to Christ clothed in what Paul calls our "old self" (i.e., with dirty clothes on). We come as we are. Paul says we are welcoming those who are deceivers (4:22), liars (4:25), people with anger issues (4:26, 31), thieves (4:28), people who are bitter (4:31), sexually immoral (5:3), etc. It sounds like this sign, just some of the examples are different. We do come just as we are, but Christ transforms us! Paul's point is this kind of life is what you *were*, but you have put off those clothes and you are now clothed in Jesus Christ. That's why he goes on to say, "Do not get drunk with wine . . . Instead, be filled with the Spirit" (Eph. 5:18). This is the language of transformation. The radical call of the New Testament it is always tied to repentance: "The kingdom of God is at hand; repent and believe the gospel" (Mark 1:15).

When I was in high school, I was on the typing team and did competitive typing across the state of Georgia. Any good typist will tell you that fast typing is possible only when your left hand and your right hand are in perfect coordination and rhythm. If 1 Corinthians 13:1 is written by only using the left hand of the typewriter keyboard, it reads like this: "f sea te tges f e r f ages bt d t ave ve a a resdg gg r a cagg cba." If you use both hands, it reads correctly: "If I speak in the tongues of men and of angels, but have not love, I am a noisy gong or a clanging cymbal."

If we only extend the radical, inclusive call, we actually speak in gibberish. Even though every stroke of the left hand was accurate, it takes both to speak with gospel coherence. Alternatively, if we focus inward and become separatists and judgmental, we can lose our heart for a lost world, and then we also speak gibberish. We become a clanging cymbal. Both of these must be brought together to speak coherently to the world about what it means to be a Christian.

## The Church as the Arena for Radical Transformation

So now we symbolically arrive at the church with all of our rags on, and we witness the transformation of the church of Jesus Christ who have availed themselves of the means of grace. When we, or *if* we, cross over and become members of the baptized community, we must take off those dirty clothes and be clothed with the garments of the church.

The metaphor of "taking off" and "putting on" is a common theme throughout Scripture. Isaiah 61:10 is one of the texts upon which the New Testament builds when it declares, "For he has clothed me with garments of salvation and arrayed me in a robe of righteousness." This metaphor is repeated throughout the New Testament, defining what it means to belong to the people of God and the new life in Jesus Christ. Here are a few examples:

> Do not lie to one other, seeing that you have put off the old self with its practices and have put on the new self, which is being renewed in knowledge after the image of its creator. (Col. 3:9–10)

> Let us cast off the works of darkness and put on the armor of light. . . . But put on the Lord Jesus Christ, and make no provision for the flesh, to gratify its desires. (Rom. 13:12, 14)

> For as many of you as were baptized into Christ have put on Christ. (Gal. 3:27)

> Therefore, since we are surrounded by so great a cloud of witnesses, let us also lay aside every weight, and sin which clings so closely, and let us run with endurance the race that is set before us, looking to

Jesus, the founder and perfecter of our faith, who for the joy that was set before him endured the cross, despising the shame, and is seated at the right hand of the throne of God. (Heb. 12:1–2)

. . . to put off your old self, which belongs to your former manner of life and is corrupt through deceitful desires, and to be renewed in the spirit of your minds, and to put on the new self, created after the likeness of God in true righteousness and holiness. (Eph. 4:22–23)

If we allow the radical, unconditional, inclusive call to be separated from the radical transformation via the new life in Christ, then we have fractured God's work and it is known as cheap grace. It is cheap grace that pretends that the first half of the gospel can be separated from the second half of the gospel and not call for transformation. This cheap grace drives a wedge between justification and sanctification and presumes upon the grace of God while we continue to live in sin. Cheap grace separates the radical call from the radical transformation.

In my youth I was a Boy Scout and loved to go cave exploring. I remember once I arrived home late on Sunday afternoon after a weekend of cave exploring. I knocked on the door, and my own mother wouldn't let me in the house! I was too filthy. She told me to leave those filthy clothes in the carport and then come in. This is a metaphor of God's own love for us. We are warmly received at the door of salvation, but the Lord says to us, in effect, "Take off those dirty clothes, and I will clothe you in the garments of Christ."

## Parable of the Prodigal Son

Remember the parable of the prodigal son in Luke 15? The younger son had taken his inheritance and went off to the far country and squandered his money with loose living and prostitutes. It is a picture of a person who has clothed himself with the world and eventually finds himself in a pig's sty, longing to eat the pods the pigs were eating. He and his clothes were filthy from wallowing with the swine. He eventually repented and returned to his father and in great humility said, "Father, I have sinned against heaven and before you. I am no longer worthy to be called your son. Treat me as one of your hired servants" (Luke 15:19). In a wonderful picture of grace, the father ran to meet him, embraced him, and reinstated him to his former position as a son (that is the radical acceptance), and then clothed him by putting a robe on him, symbolic of the transformation that happens when we come to Christ in repentance (Luke 15:22). Perhaps the sign on the church should have concluded with the verse, "If anyone is in Christ, he is a new creation. The old has passed away; behold, the new has come" (2 Cor. 5:17).

The radical call of the gospel should never be leveraged against the holiness that characterizes the church of Jesus Christ. It is a false narrative that if we speak of holiness we are denying the radical embracing love of Jesus Christ! Paul makes it very clear that those who live in darkness cannot inherit the kingdom of God (Eph. 5:5). We are a transformed community. As we cross over and become full members of the baptized community of the people of God, we are a peculiar people clothed in righteousness and holiness. When we come to Christ, we bring with us all the same muddled thinking and unholy lives that the world has, and Christ Himself sets out to transform us by His very divine presence. He has chosen the church to be a key instrument—a means of grace for that transformation. Transformation is never bad news; it is part of the good news, because it is a call to human flourishing.

Even if the sign on the church were left as it is, perhaps the back of the sign should read like this when you leave the church: "But you are a chosen people, a royal priesthood, a holy nation, a people for his own possession, that you may proclaim the excellencies of him who called you out of darkness into his marvelous light" (1 Peter 2:9).

## The Church as Sealed in the Means of Grace by the Spirit of God

Finally, Paul reminds us that the Holy Spirit is the seal of the means of grace. Without the Spirit we end up with either legalism or the collapse of holiness. In Ephesians 4:30 Paul turns to the third person of the Trinity when he says, "Do not grieve the Holy Spirit of God, by whom you were sealed for the day of redemption." In 5:18 he commands us, "Be filled with the [Holy] Spirit." Why the transition to the Holy Spirit? The Holy Spirit is particularly grieved when we walk as the world walks because the Holy Spirit is the primary agent of our sanctification. The Holy Spirit has been charged to empower us as Christ's sanctified church. Without the Spirit we cannot live in the grace of God. We must never forget that the operative word in the phrase "means of grace" is *grace*. God does something in us that we cannot accomplish through our own strength. There is an old poem that beautifully sums up the powerlessness of the Law to make us holy compared to the inner work of the Holy Spirit. It goes like this:

> *To work and to run the law demands;*
> *But gives us neither feet nor hands;*
> *Better news the gospel brings,*
> *It bids us fly and gives us wings!*

The gospel has an even higher standard than the Old Testament law and yet gives us the power to live it out! This is not self-empowered holy living but a holiness enabled through the power of the Holy Spirit. Paul goes on to highlight three examples of what we are to "put off" (Eph. 4:22) if we are to be followers of Christ: corrupting talk (4:29), unforgiveness (4:32), and sexual immorality (5:3). Just think what a radiant light the church would be if just those three things were embodied by the church: truth and wholesome speech, not crude discourse; forgiveness, not harboring bitterness and unforgiveness; and sexual purity, not sexual immorality. If we, through the power of the Spirit of God, were to manifest those three admonitions, then the beauty of the Christian community would almost instantly rise up above this culture in stunning ways. We would actually be on our way to embodying a holy community who exemplifies both the radical call and the radical transformation.

◆ Chapter Two ◆

# Baptism as a Means of Grace

*The Four Stories of Baptism*

SCRIPTURAL BACKGROUND: ROMANS 6:1–14

If you were to visit my office at Asbury Theological Seminary, you would see a picture on the wall with four pivotal quotes from church history. These quotations are daily reminders to me that our own place in church history is defined by moments of faithfulness where we are tested and God gives us the grace to say or do the right thing. The first of the four sayings comes from Martin Luther in 1521. Following Luther's confession of his faith in Christ alone, his followers, in fear that Luther would be killed, hid him in Wartburg Castle for ten months. It is there that Luther reportedly threw an inkwell at the devil (visitors to the castle can still see the ink stain on the wall). In my mind, it is not whether or not Luther threw the inkwell at the devil that is important but what he said when he threw it. This statement is the first quote on my wall: "*Baptizatus sum!*"

It means "I am baptized!" Luther did not say that he *was* baptized but that he *is* baptized, meaning that he currently stood as a baptized member of the church of Jesus Christ. In this chapter we will explore baptism as a means of grace.

Baptism is the means of grace that stands at the seam between the old life and the new life, the radical call and the radical transformation we explored in the last chapter. Baptism is the doorway between our unregenerate life in the old Adam and our regenerate new life in the second Adam. The New Testament is filled with baptisms! Three thousand were baptized on the day of Pentecost, the birthday of the church (Acts 2:41). As we turn the pages of Acts, we read about the Samaritan believers being baptized (8:12), the Ethiopian eunuch (8:38), and the baptism of Saul of Tarsus (9:18), who becomes known to us as the apostle Paul. We see many households being baptized, including the households of Cornelius (10:47–48), Lydia (16:15), the Philippian jailer (16:30), and Crispus, the synagogue ruler (18:8). We see new churches being established through baptism, in Ephesus and Corinth (18:8; 19:5). One might say that the book of Acts is really a long story of baptisms, one after another. It is the great mark of Christian identity.

Our scriptural passage from Romans 6 should not be isolated out as a text about baptism without seeing it within the larger context of Paul's argument. In chapter 5, Paul has been talking about how sin and death entered the world through Adam. This is the "old self," which Paul tells us must be "put off." But the point of Romans 5 is to demonstrate that just as *sin, death, and condemnation* spread to the entire human race through the first Adam, now, in Christ, *righteousness, reconciliation, and eternal life* are spreading to the entire human race through Jesus Christ, the second Adam. Baptism is introduced in Romans 6 not as a new topic, or a new theme, but as the sign or seal of this transition from the old life in the first Adam to the new life in the second Adam, Jesus Christ. Baptism is the sign of being "in Christ," whereas before we were "in Adam." Because Paul has been extolling the power of God's radical grace, he is concerned that (just as it has happened in the contemporary church) the doctrine of grace and the inclusive embrace of God could be interpreted as a license to sin.

So, Paul opens the chapter by asking, "What shall we say then? Are we to continue in sin that grace may abound? By no means! How can we who died to sin still live in it?" (Rom. 6:1–2). It is here that Paul introduces baptism. It actually comes as a bit of a surprise, because I think given the content of the letter to the Romans you might expect him to say, "Do you not know that all of us who have put our faith in Jesus Christ have been united to His death, and through faith we are united to His resurrection?" But, Paul doesn't use the word *faith*. Instead, he turns to the sacrament of baptism (Rom. 6:3–4).

When we think about baptism, our minds quickly go to all of the controversial questions that have divided the church: What is the meaning of baptism? What is the proper mode of baptism? Who is eligible to be baptized, infants or believing adults? What precisely should be said in terms of baptismal formula? Should we be baptized in the name of the triune God or just in the name of Jesus? Is it a sacrament or an ordinance? Is it a sign or a seal? On and on the questions come. But, our very differences underscore how important and central the doctrine is in the life of the church. It is easy to get distracted by the various disputes about baptism in the church and miss the fact that this is actually one of the great *unifying* features of the church.

If you take time to study every text in the New Testament that teaches about baptism, you will discover that the meaning of baptism is unfolded through the lens of four stories. In this chapter, we will look at these four baptism stories, which illuminate four metaphors, all pointing to one transformation. Only by understanding all four metaphors or stories do we actually begin to understand the full meaning of baptism.

## Four Metaphors—One Transformation

### (1) Noah and the Ark: Baptism as Sign of Spiritual Cleansing and New Birth

The first story is the story of Noah and the ark. Most of us know from our Sunday school days the amazing story of how God delivered Noah and his family from the waters of destruction through the ark. What you may not know is that all throughout church history the ark has been used by Christians as a symbol of the church. Just as Noah's ark was used to deliver Noah from judgment and through those waters into salvation, so the church is the means by which those who believe in and confess Christ are delivered from judgment and into the salvation offered through Jesus

35

Christ. So, in the New Testament even the waters that Noah was carried through become a symbol of the waters of baptism. Just as Noah was brought to a new life after the flood, so we are brought to a new life after our baptism.

Peter teaches this in his first epistle when he speaks of

the days of Noah, while the ark was being prepared, in which a few, that is, eight persons, were brought safely through water. Baptism, which corresponds to this, now saves you, not as a removal of dirt from the body but as an appeal to God for a good conscience, through the resurrection of Jesus Christ, who has gone into heaven and is at the right hand of God, with angels, authorities, and powers having been subjected to him. (1 Peter 3:20–22)

The water of our baptism, whether we were sprinkled or immersed, is a symbol of our trusting in God to save us through judgment, just as Noah trusted God when the flood came. The use of water also resonates with a number of other water images in the Old Testament. First, there are the primordial waters of Genesis out of which God brought His creation into order (Gen. 1:2). Just as God brought life out of that "void and darkness" and "waters," so God uses our baptism to serve as a kind of new creation day. It is like getting to go back to the beginning and start all over again. What a great gift this is! Second, the Jewish priests used water for their own cleansing before a sacrifice (Lev. 16:4). Thus, early on water became a symbol of cleansing. To this day we use water to clean things. Third, the real birth of the Jewish people happened when they left their Egyptian bondage behind and crossed through the Red Sea. The passing through the waters of the Red Sea has long symbolized baptism as we leave behind our bondage to the old life and cross over through the waters of baptism to the new promised land of grace and salvation. Finally, we were all physically born out of the water of our mother's womb. Thus, baptism is like being reborn through water into our new life in Jesus Christ. While all of these images of water are important, we are focusing here on the story of Noah and the ark and the waters of that judgment out of which he was saved. When you are baptized and join the church, it is like entering into the ark through which God saves His redeemed children.

## (2) Israel Circumcised in the Wilderness: Baptism as the Sign of the Covenant

The second story is the story of the children of Israel being circumcised in the wilderness. The familiar phrase

"Old Testament" really means the "Old Covenant." The story of the Old Testament is the story of God entering into covenant with the Jewish people in order to reveal His saving purposes for the whole human race. This goes all the way back to Genesis 12 where God first enters into a covenant with Abraham. In that passage God declares that He will make Abraham a great nation and give the Jewish people land and inheritance, and ultimately through Abraham all nations will be blessed (Gen. 12:1–3). Years later the covenant was established with the Jewish people by bringing them through the Red Sea and to Mt. Sinai where they received the Law. It was important that those who entered into a covenant with God would be marked with a sign or seal that testified to the relationship they had with God. The sign of the covenant was circumcision. So, Abraham and his family were circumcised (Gen. 17:9–14), and later the Jewish nation who received the Ten Commandments were circumcised (Ex. 12:43–48). Finally, the new generation that entered the promised land were also circumcised (Josh. 5:2–7).

In the New Testament, baptism became our outward and visible sign of our covenant with God just as circumcision was for the Jewish people of the Old Testament. Thus, the story of the children of Israel being circumcised becomes one of the key stories used in the New Testament to explain the meaning of baptism. Paul makes the connection very clear in Colossians 2:11–12 when he says, "In him [Jesus Christ] also you were circumcised with a circumcision made without hands, by putting off the body of the flesh, by the circumcision of Christ, having been buried with him in baptism, in which you were also raised with him through faith in the powerful working of God, who raised him from the dead." He makes a similar point in Romans 4:10–12. Thus, baptism becomes the outward sign or seal of God's covenant with us as the people of God.

### (3) The Death and Resurrection of Christ: Baptism as Being Buried and Raised with Christ

There is little doubt that the cross has become the central symbol of the Christian faith. You can find crosses on the roofs of our church buildings, on the altars of our churches, and on chains around our necks. The cross, of course, was nothing more than a particularly cruel and gruesome form of execution in the ancient world. However, it is revered by Christians because it tells a story. It tells the story of our redemption through the death and resurrection of Jesus

Christ. He died for our sins and He was raised to newness of life. This is the third story that baptism symbolizes. Just as Christ was buried and raised, when we go down into the waters of baptism, we are symbolically going down into a grave where we die to our sins, and when we come up out of the water, we are symbolically raised with Christ to our new life.

The connection of our baptism with Christ's own death and resurrection is one of the most cherished stories of the Christian faith. Paul makes this connection in both his epistles to the Romans and to the Colossians. He tells believers at Colossae that they "have been buried with him [Christ] in baptism, in which you were also raised with him through faith in the powerful working of God, who raised him from the dead" (Col. 2:12). To the Romans, Paul declares, "Do you not know that all of us who have been baptized into Christ Jesus were baptized into his death? We were therefore buried with him through baptism into death, in order that, just as Christ was raised from the dead by the glory of the Father, we too might walk in newness of life" (Rom. 6:3–4). Baptism is a symbol of the grave and our union with Christ as we share in His death (we die to our sins) and His resurrection (we become partakers of the new life).

## (4) Being Clothed: The Story of Christian Conversion

The fourth and final story is the great story of Christian conversion through the metaphor of becoming clothed with Christ. In the early church when someone emerged from the waters of baptism (usually on Easter Sunday), they would be clothed in a white robe. This symbolized the new life they were taking on in Jesus Christ. They had put off the old self and put on the new self in Jesus Christ. This image is also used by the apostle Paul. He tells the Galatian Christians, "For as many of you as were were baptized into Christ have put on Christ" (Gal. 3:27). Similar statements are found in other places in the New Testament (Rom. 13:14; Eph. 4:22–23; Col. 3:9; Heb. 12:1–2). The taking off of our old clothes refers to all of the sins and bondages of the old life, whereas the putting on of our new clothes refers to the new life we now have in Jesus Christ. Conversion is the bridge between the old life and the new life. Paul, for example, says, "Let us walk properly as in the daytime, not in orgies and drunkenness, not in sexual immorality and sensuality, not in quarreling and jealousy. But put on the Lord Jesus Christ, and make no provision for the flesh, to gratify its desires" (Rom. 13:13–14).

These four stories each shed a special light on the sacrament of baptism. The fact that there are four rather different stories provides some explanation as to why churches differ in how they understand baptism. If you emphasize the first two stories (Noah and the ark; the children of Israel getting circumcised), you tend to baptize infants and sprinkle rather than immerse, and the sacrament is understood as a mark of the covenant. In other words, it is more about God's action than our decision-making. If you emphasize the latter two stories (death and resurrection of Christ; clothing and unclothing as a sign of Christian conversion), you lean toward seeing baptism as an expression of individual faith, and, therefore, you tend to emphasize believing adults immersed in full water (which is the best imagery of a death and resurrection) and downplay the sacramental aspect of the act (perhaps calling it an ordinance rather than a sacrament). However, we need all four stories, as each one gives us a glimpse into the theology of baptism. The apostle Paul, after all, is the author of three of the four, so we should not pit one against the other, or emphasize one over the other. Rather, *we are to always hear all four stories.*

This is what keeps baptism as a means of grace. It reminds us of our status, and it interweaves us into God's larger redemptive stories (Noah, nation of Israel, Christ's own death and resurrection, conversion and clothing of the people of God), reminding us that baptism is never merely an individual act of faith, but we are baptized *into a faith*. Baptism connects us with others throughout the world and back through time. Therefore, we don't just remember our baptism as a past event; rather, we recognize that even now it unites us with all those around the world who are baptized and represent the very body of Christ in the world. This is why Luther said, "I *am* baptized" not "I *was* baptized" that day in 1521 when he threw an inkwell at the devil. We have all been marked by baptism. We have been delivered out of the waters of destruction, marked as those in covenant with God, who have died and been raised with Christ and have put on His righteousness and holiness as we go out into the world. What a wonderful means of grace this is for us all.

◆ Chapter Three ◆

# The Lord's Supper as a Means of Grace

SCRIPTURAL BACKGROUND: MATTHEW 26:26–30

Bob Stamps, former dean of the chapel at Asbury Theological Seminary, once told the true story of when he was a little boy and asked his Methodist grandmother what Methodists believed about the Lord's Supper. Bob said his grandmother shook her head and said, "I don't really know for sure. I just know we believe more than the Baptists, but less than the Catholics." If the truth were told, this expresses more than we want to admit about our understanding of the Lord's Supper. We just don't know for sure.

The purpose of this chapter is to explain what we believe about the Lord's Supper and how it serves as a means

45

of grace for us and the world. But, before we begin, it might be helpful to explain why even though almost all Christians celebrate this sacrament, they refer to it by a wide variety of terms. The three most common names are the Eucharist, Communion, and the Lord's Supper. The word *Eucharist* is taken from the Greek word for "thanksgiving," and it reflects the central part of the liturgy known as "The Great Thanksgiving." This is based on the scriptural account of when Jesus instituted the sacrament. The account says, "And when he had given thanks . . ." (Matt. 26:27; Mark 14:23; Luke 22:19; 1 Cor. 11:24). Thus, giving thanks is at the heart of the celebration. Other churches call it *Communion*, which is a Latin word meaning "sharing" or "mutual participation," and it reflects that we are brought together in a spiritual way with Christ and one another during the sacrament. This term is also found in Scripture when Paul says in 1 Corinthians 10:16 that the cup is a "participation" in the blood of Christ and the bread is a "participation" in the body of Christ. In other translations of the passage, the word *participation* is translated as "fellowship" or "communion." The third term, the *Lord's Supper*, is taken directly from Scripture since Paul refers to it as such (1 Cor. 11:20). Thus, all three terms are taken from Scripture, and we should therefore be familiar with all of them.

The best way to get into the meaning of the Lord's Supper is to look at it through three lenses. Each of the three lenses allows us to look in three distinct directions—the past, present, and future. Only by looking in all three directions can we properly capture the meaning of the Eucharist.

## Looking through the Past Lens

This "looking back" lens begins by remembering that Jesus instituted the sacrament of the Lord's Supper at the Jewish Passover. This was very intentional by Jesus. The Passover meal was the annual commemoration of the Jews celebrating and remembering God's dramatic intervention in saving the children of Israel out of the bondage of Egyptian slavery. The Jews would partake of a meal that remembered and reenacted what God did that first Passover night when the blood of the lamb spared them from the judgment of death. In the same way, when we take the Lord's Supper, we look back on our redemption from spiritual bondage. Jesus Christ inaugurated a new Passover. The second way the Lord's Supper points us backward is, of course, in the actual death of Jesus Christ on the cross. When we take the Lord's Supper, we look back on Jesus' death on the cross, as well as His resurrection, ascension, and enthronement at the right hand of God the Father. This is the reminder of Jesus' victory over sin and death. The third way we look to the past is that the Lord's Supper is meant to remind us of our own baptism into new life. In other words, the story of redemption from the early Jewish Passover that prefigured the coming of Jesus into the world and Jesus' work on the cross are not events disconnected from our lives. Through baptism and participation in the Lord's Supper, we are brought into this great redemptive story. We become part of it. We are not just remembering past acts of salvation, but our own salvation and participation in God's unfolding plan to reconcile all things to Himself. God has delivered *you* from bondage and brought *you* into His adoptive family. This is the amazing truth of this past lens.

## Looking through the Present Lens

When we come forward to take the Lord's Supper, we believe that it is more than just a memorial or memory of past events of redemption. It is here that Christians begin to disagree about the meaning of the sacrament. Some Christians only look through the lens of the past.

But, through the present lens we discover that Christ actually meets us at the table and is spiritually present with us to convey His grace and forgiveness. This is actually not so much tied to anything that happens to the elements of bread and cup as it is to the very presence of Christ as the host of this sacred meal of fellowship. This is where the phrase "Lord's Table" or "Lord's Supper" is important. The table spread does not belong to any denomination or any group of Christians. We are not the host; Jesus Christ is the host. We cannot absolve people of their sins; only He can. The real presence of Jesus in the sacraments is taken from Jesus' own words, "This is my body" and "This is my blood." He does not say, "This *represents* my body." The presence of Jesus is also understood from Paul's use of the word *Communion*, which we noted earlier in the chapter. The Lord's Supper is more than receiving forgiveness (as wonderful as that is). It is also communion with Christ Himself, who is mystically present with us. The presence of Christ at the table is what led John Wesley to practice what is known as "open" Communion, meaning anyone can come forward to receive. If the Lord's Supper only remembers past acts of redemption, then, of course, only baptized believers in full fellowship of the church should come forward to receive. But if Christ Himself is present, then He invites all to Himself. Someone could, Wesley reasoned, get out of their pew to come forward as an unbeliever and actually meet and receive the good news of the gospel in the very presence of Jesus Himself. This is where we really begin to see the power of the Lord's Supper as a converting sacrament. It has the power to convert people to the faith. Some people best hear the gospel through words, such as through a sermon, while others hear the gospel through the tangible, physical touch of the bread and wine. Charles Wesley captured this powerfully when he wrote, "Come, Sinners, to the Gospel Feast, let every soul be Jesus' guest. Ye need not one be left behind, for God hath bid all humankind."[2]

The Lord's Supper is also present for those of us who are baptized believers. The elements declare afresh our forgiveness and our solidarity with Christ through this covenant established through His shed blood. Through the Lord's Supper the power of the death and resurrection of Christ is communicated afresh to us and we are reconciled to God and to one another.

The Lord's Supper is also present with us as we go out into the world. The sacrament transforms us as we go

---

2. Charles Wesley, "Come, Sinners to the Gospel Feast," *The Asbury Hymnal* (Franklin, TN: Seedbed, 2018), 234.

forth to give our lives to a world in need. The words of Christ "This is my body, given for you" become our own words to the world as we say, through acts of service and love, "This is my body, given for you." We become sacramentally present to the world in the here and now as the transformed people of God.

## Looking through the Lens of the Future

The Lord's Supper also is a pointer to future realities. We have already seen how the Lord's Supper is another way the church proclaims the gospel. The sacraments are very different than preaching. Preaching is the Word that goes forth and strikes the ears of the world and the believing community. The Lord's Supper visibly demonstrates the gospel and is not just an *ear* witness but an *eye* witness of the mystery of the gospel. It is not just something we say; it is something we do. But, it also compels us to look forward to a day when this broken world will be healed. The Lord's Supper is a regular reminder to ourselves and to the world that the kingdom has not yet fully come. We do not live in a perfect world, but a fallen world. Our world is full of sin and fallenness, and we eagerly await the visible, bodily return of Christ. Paul himself testifies about this when he says in reference to the Lord's Supper, "For as often as you eat this bread and drink the cup, you proclaim the Lord's death until he comes" (1 Cor. 11:26).

The Lord's Supper is a proclamation of His death until His bodily return. Every time we share in the Lord's Supper, we do not only look back and remember our past redemption, nor do we only receive Christ's forgiveness and grace as He walks with us right now, today. It is also a testimony to future realities. By faith we look forward to the culmination of this great story of redemption when Christ returns and fully consummates His kingdom. One of the high points of the Communion liturgy is when we say as a congregation: Christ has died (past), Christ is risen (present), and Christ will come again (future). We look to that day when Christ will fully consummate His kingdom. We currently live in the tension between the already and the not yet. The rule and reign of God has already broken into our lives and into the world, but it is clearly not yet consummated. Someday, all the enemies of Christ will be put under His feet and the kingdom of God will be fully realized. The Scriptures teach that the culmination of the ages and the consummation of the kingdom will be accompanied by a great banquet, a feast with all of God's people through the ages, including Abraham, Isaac, and Jacob (Matt. 8:11; Rev. 19:9). This banquet will also include the thief on the cross and all of us sinners who, by grace, have received the good news of the kingdom. It is known as the Marriage Supper of the Lamb (Rev. 19:9). This is the great moment at the climax of the ages when all the realities of the new creation will be fully revealed. There will be new heavens and a new earth. All will be restored. The biggest transformation will be the absence of sin and the full manifestation of the eternal presence of Christ.

The elements of the Lord's Supper are actually connected to this larger feast at the end of time. You should see the elements of the Lord's Supper (bread and wine) as the hors d'oeuvres in anticipation of the larger feast to come. In fact, the early church often connected the Lord's Supper with a larger love feast to demonstrate in a more obvious way that the church is headed to that future day when we will enjoy a beautiful celebrative banquet together.

## Lord's Supper as a Means of Grace

The purpose of this chapter is about more than explaining the meaning of the Lord's Supper it is also to illustrate how God has instituted it as a means of grace. There are three important ways in which God's grace is conveyed to us through this sacrament.

*First, the Lord has instituted the sacrament to convey the truth and power of the work of Jesus Christ in our lives.* One of the wonderful things about the sacrament is its physical, tangible, tactile nature. One might be able to passively listen to a sermon or a choral anthem, but the sacrament of the Lord's Supper calls for us to walk forward and eat and drink something. It is something we *do*, not merely something we *hear*. It is simultaneously ordinary and extraordinary. We eat multiple times per day, but we also realize Jesus conveyed something extraordinary when He said, "Whoever eats my flesh and drinks my blood remains in me, and I in him" (John 6:56). The physical elements of bread and wine are, at the least, tangible reminders of the physical reality of the incarnation and the real sacrifice of the body of Jesus for the sins of the world, not to mention the physical reality of the bodily resurrection, which confirms and testifies to His victory over sin and death.

This is why the death and resurrection of Jesus can never be reduced to a mere symbolic victory that is not rooted in the actual historical, physical death and resurrection of Jesus. The physicality of the elements stands as a pointer to something that truly and physically happened in history. Therefore, it stands as a means of grace to us. It is beyond the purpose of this chapter to explore how different churches view what may or may not happen to the elements used in the Lord's Supper. The point I am trying to make is that we should not focus so much on what change happens to the elements but on the change that happens in us because Christ is present. He is the real host of the supper, and it is a meal in His honor. Jesus is truly present at the Lord's Supper. We may not agree on how He is present, but the point is that wherever Jesus is, transformation can occur. This is why we noted in the first chapter that Jesus is the fountainhead of all the means of grace. The Lord's Supper is a means of grace, but only because Christ makes it so through His presence at the sacred meal. However, there is a second dimension to the sacrament as a means of grace that is often overlooked.

*This sacrament is given as a sign of reconciliation.* When we come forward to receive the Lord's Supper, we normally think about it as something that God does *for* us in setting things right between ourselves and God. Indeed, we do receive the grace of Christ as we partake of the Lord's Supper. However, if you listen to the liturgy carefully, the sacrament is not merely vertical (i.e., about our personal relationship with God); it is also horizontal. It conveys a powerful grace to reconcile us with one another. The sacrament is rooted and grounded in reconciliation. This is why

Paul admonishes the Christians in Corinth to not partake of the Lord's Supper if they are quarreling with one another and the church is divided: "I hear that there are divisions among you. . . . When you come together, it is not the Lord's supper that you eat" (1 Cor. 11:18–20). Rather than it being a means of grace, they were actually eating and drinking judgment on themselves (1 Cor. 11:29). Thus, the sacrament is a means of grace not only for our own reception of forgiveness but also our reconciliation with our neighbor. Yet, even this is not the full extent and power of the sacrament as a means of grace. There is a third dimension which is more missional and external.

*The sacrament of the Lord's Supper should be a means of grace to the unbelieving world.* It is hard for us to imagine that a sacrament could somehow serve an unbelieving world. However, we must always remember that when we as the people of God embody forgiveness and grace, we become a beacon of hope for a broken world. Immediately after Paul speaks about the reconciling work of Christ on the cross, he goes on to say, "Therefore, we are ambassadors for Christ, God making his appeal though us. We implore you on behalf of Christ, be reconciled to God" (2 Cor. 5:20). This is a stunning statement. Paul is saying that we are the very channels through which God makes His appeal to the world to be reconciled to God. Therefore, our own transformation and reconciliation, effected through the sacrament, is a means of grace to the world. We hear quite a bit today about the need for racial reconciliation and addressing deep, systemic issues that go back for hundreds of years in our country. We must remember that the government has a very short arm when it comes to addressing these kinds of issues. Governments are good at passing laws, but they cannot reach into the human heart. God has a very long arm when it comes to addressing the issues our culture, or any culture, faces. God, through the power of the cross, the ministry of reconciliation, and the outpouring of the Holy Spirit can transform any heart and bring about deep, lasting change.

## Conclusion

This chapter has presented three lenses that help us look to the past, the present, and the future as we reflect on the mystery of the Lord's Supper. These should not be viewed as any kind of comprehensive explanation of the sacrament, but more like insights into a mystery. It is important to remember that the word *sacrament* literally means "holy mystery," and we should always keep that in mind as we reflect on the sacraments. We have also seen that this sacrament is a means of grace for us as not only we receive forgiveness and grace but also as we extend grace to our neighbors, and ultimately, as we bear witness of the gospel to the ends of the earth. We do not just take sacraments; we embody them as the reconciled people of God.

This chapter is just a brief primer to help you on a lifelong journey that draws you deeper into this great mystery, which is only fully known and understood in the presence of Christ Himself.

# Chapter Four

# Prayer as a Means of Grace

In 1984, I was in my first appointment as a young pastor in the North Georgia Conference of the United Methodist Church. I learned early on that pastors were required to get a certain number of Continuing Education Units (CEUs) each year. I was eager to find out how to sign up because I was committed to lifelong learning. I found out that each year the conference officially sponsored a CEU event, and it was expected that everyone would attend that training to keep their ordinations current. So, at a district meeting in 1984, my district superintendent passed around the brochure highlighting the officially sponsored

1984 CEU training for the conference. I eagerly took one of the brochures. Across the front of the brochure was emblazoned: "Lord, Teach Us to Pray." My mind immediately went to that line from the disciples taken right out of Luke 11:1, and I began to think how much I needed to grow in my prayer life. Then, I suddenly realized that there was a huge misprint on the brochure. The brochure actually said, "Lord, Teach Us to Play." I quickly opened up the brochure to look at the sessions, and I realized that it was not an error at all, but it was a—no pun intended—word play off of Luke 11:1, and the CEU was actually dedicated to helping pastors cultivate time for play in their lives. Certainly, there are pastors who are workaholics, and it may be important to help some pastors learn how to relax, develop boundaries to their professional lives, and learn how to play. But, even by 1984, the culture was already awash with entertainment, admonitions for boundary keeping, self-care, and play. I determined right then and there, even though I was a junior member of the conference, I was not going to spend a week on a conference entitled "Lord, Teach Us to Play." I approached the district superintendent and asked if I could fulfill the requirement through some other event and he agreed, as long as it was approved by the denomination. Now, I faced a dilemma because I had already scheduled those particular days to be off, including a Sunday morning. So, I needed to find an approved continuing education event that was taking place on that very week. After considerable searching (don't forget, this is before the days of the internet), I found one event available in Atlanta on that weekend that was an approved CEU event, led by a United Methodist named Terry Teykl from Texas. To my utter amazement, the title of the event was "Lord, Teach Us to Pray." This is one of those stories that many of us have in life where, when you tell it, you realize that it is almost unbelievable. I was supposed to go to a conference entitled "Lord, Teach Us to Play," and God sovereignly brought me to a conference entitled "Lord, Teach Us to Pray." As it turned out, that conference was a major turning point in my life and ministry. It was at that conference that I was introduced to a book by Dick Eastman entitled *The Hour That Changes the World.* That little book was a life-changer for me. I am convinced that my nearly forty-year ministry as a pastor, a missionary, a seminary professor, and now a seminary president would have not unfolded as it did had it not been for that weekend where I learned more deeply about the practice of prayer.

Some of you know that the entire struggle over the person of Christ in the fifth century came down to two words with only a one-letter difference (*Homoousion*, meaning same substance or essence, and *homoiousion*, meaning like, or similar, substance or essence). It is hard to imagine it, but the whole of our Christology hinged on that one letter. As it turned out, much of my life and ministry hinged on the tiny-one letter difference between the words *play* and *pray*.

This chapter is dedicated to prayer as a means of grace and will focus on the necessity of developing personal, persistent prayer in our lives. We will devote the next chapter to the Lord's Prayer. These two chapters will serve together to capture a glimpse of the power of prayer as a means of grace.

Our focal point for this meditation will be Luke 18:1–8, which is a parable about persistence. This is one of my favorite parables in Luke's gospel, because it not only carries an amazing and powerful message for the church, but it is delivered in a way that demonstrates what a powerful teacher Jesus is. Jesus uses an ingenious method of teaching not through a series of comparisons, which one might expect, but through a series of insightful contrasts to make His point.

The parable unfolds around two main characters, a judge and a widow. Jesus describes this judge as one who neither feared God nor man. By this description we can surmise that this judge was an unbeliever, without a heart for justice, even on a humanistic level, and was likely appointed for political reasons, rather than for his integrity or the wisdom of his insights. Jesus is picturing a man here who is aloof and unconcerned about justice. How would you feel if you knew your case, upon which your life depended, would be brought before such a man, with no recourse for justice and no right of appeal?

Jesus goes on to highlight the second character in the story, a helpless widow from that same town. In the Jewish culture of the day and throughout the ancient world, a widow epitomizes helplessness and vulnerability. A widow was generally forced to go back to her father's house for protection. There was no welfare net, no child support, no department of family and children services. Nothing. There were very few ways any single woman could support herself in the first century, and a widow such as this would be vulnerable to exploitation. The people listening to Jesus' message understood that this widow had been exploited and deprived of justice.

When her husband died, she probably had a clear deed to some property, but in the ancient world when your husband died, someone might come and just occupy the property. This is exactly what Ahab did to Naboth's property in 1 Kings 21. Or, it could have been that some-body owed her husband a sum of money, and it was rightfully hers now that her husband was dead.

We don't know the exact circumstances, but we do know that she was being cheated and her only recourse was to go before this unjust judge. There were no other options in the system.

*This unjust judge was her only hope.* So the widow comes to the judge and asks him to administer justice on her behalf. The judge refuses this widow with no social standing; after all, a widow was a nobody in the ancient world. That's why the Scriptures are full of texts where God commands His people to look after orphans and widows, because if God's people don't, few others will.

This widow is pictured by Jesus as someone who lacks everything she needs in terms of resources, legal or cultural options, respect, etc. But, there was one thing she did have—persistence! Her persistence is the focal point of the parable. This widow would not be denied justice and did not relent until justice was served. She goes back to the judge again and again and again, saying, "Give me justice against my adversary" (Luke 18:3).

For a time, the unjust judge who neither feared God nor man gave no regard to a widow without status in society and ignored her plea. But she kept coming back to the judge, over and over again, and eventually her persistence wore him down. He said, "I will give her justice, so that she will not beat me down with her continual coming" (Luke 18:5). Essentially, he said, "I've got to get this woman off my back." The great sixteenth-century Reformer Martin Luther translated this verse as "Give her what she wants so she won't deafen me!"

It is clear from the outset of the parable that this is a parable about prayer. In fact, the opening line makes this clear when we are told that Jesus told them this parable in order that "they ought always to pray and not lose heart" (Luke 18:1).

Notice how Jesus teaches by way of contrasts. If even this unjust judge answers the widow, then *how much more so* will God answer the prayers of the persistent. The point of the parable is driven home by a range of contrasts.

The judge was unjust, but the Lord is just. The judge had no concern for justice, but the Lord is the very embodiment of justice and righteousness. The judge didn't want to listen to the woman's case; he would rather to have never have laid eyes upon her. In contrast, the Lord says, "Call to me and I will answer you" (Jer. 33:3). The judge was aloof and unconcerned about her plight. But, Jesus says, "Come to me, all who labor and are heavy laden, and I will give you rest" (Matt. 11:28). The judge had no desire to support the widow in her cause. The Scripture says, "The eyes of the LORD run to and fro throughout the whole earth, to give strong support to those whose heart is blameless toward him" (2 Chron. 16:9). The point is that if this unjust, wicked, aloof judge who feared neither God nor man eventually granted her request, then how much more so will the Lord of Glory listen to His children who call upon His name.

In addition to the contrast between the unjust judge and an attentive and loving heavenly Father, another contrast in this parable should not be missed. Jesus is not only contrasting the *judge* with God, He is also contrasting the *widow* with the church. The widow had no legal standing or rights in her society, but the church has a legal standing before God, as we are the blood-bought, redeemed, adopted, sealed, and set-apart children of God. The widow had no reason for confidence, but the church is told to confidently "draw near to the throne of grace, that we may receive mercy and find grace to help in time of need" (Heb. 4:16), and that we are no longer strangers but heirs of the Father, joint heirs with the Son (Eph. 2:19; Rom. 8:17). Therefore, if the widow with no legal standing was heard, *how much more so* will God heed our prayers? This is why Jesus uses "chosen ones" in verse 7. How much more so will "God give justice to his elect, who cry to him day and night?" (Luke 18:7).

This text gives us three insights about persistent prayer, each demonstrating prayer as a means of grace.

The first insight is wonderfully summarized by Dick Eastman in that little classic, *The Hour That Changes the World*. Eastman wrote, "Prayer is man's ultimate indication of trust in his heavenly Father. Only in prayer do we surrender our problems completely to God and ask for divine intervention."[3] Prayer is the sign and seal of where our trust is founded and positions us before God and before one another. It is one of the greatest gifts we have been given as the people of God, which is why persistent prayer is a means of grace. We learn to trust God as we travail with one another in prayer, and through persistence, our hearts are knit individually and collectively to the heart of God. Most Christians only know casual prayer—prayer before a meal or a quick prayer to start the day—but persistent prayer is the effectual means of grace. Think about this.

---

3. Dick Eastman, *The Hour That Changes the World: A Practical Plan for Personal Prayer* (Grand Rapids, MI: Baker Publishing Group, 2002), 18.

*Persistent prayer, by definition, means unanswered prayer.*
The very fact that the widow kept returning over and over
to the judge reminds us that we live in that liminal place,
that vulnerable spot where the agony of unanswered prayer
calls for persistence.

The Psalms are full of these kind of prayers of holy
desperation. Indeed, persistence and unanswered prayer are
two sides of the same coin of trust. We learn that God is
not like Santa Claus where we climb into His lap, make
our requests, and they appear beneath the Christmas tree
before the month is out. That is a vending-machine view of
prayer. The widow teaches us that persistent prayer brings
us into a much more turbulent place of wrestling with
God, learning to trust, and growing in our capacity to wait.

The second insight is wonderfully summarized by
Blaise Pascal who said, "God instituted prayer to communicate to creatures the dignity of causality."[4] Prayer is
not simply an information session whereby we give God
information about our lives or about a situation we are
facing that He does not already know about. God already
knows every intimate detail of our lives. God has the

---

4. Blaise Pascal, *The Thoughts of Blaise Pascal*, trans. C. Kegan Paul
(London: George Bell and Sons, 1901), 298. This is from the M. Auguste
Molinier edition.

power to change every heart, solve every political crisis, right every wrong, balance every injustice, etc. So, why doesn't He just act? Scripture teaches us that there will come a day when God comes to set all things right, vindicate those who have put their faith in Him, and judge the world. But, in the meantime, we live in this liminal space between what is and what will be. We live in that sometimes uncomfortable zone between the secured victory of the resurrection and the final consummation at the end of time when all things will be made right. He wants us, through our prayers, to become part of His victory. When He finally sets things right, He wants us to share in the joy of knowing that we were part of how that victory was extended. This sacred truth never robs God of His sovereignty, but it does demonstrate that God wants us to be a part of His cosmic victory! This is what led Charles Spurgeon, a firm believer in the power and sovereignty of God, to declare that "prayer is the slender nerve that moves the mighty muscle of God's omnipotence."[5] It is prayer and the power of the causality that it unleashes in the heart and plans of God that caused Mary Queen

5. Charles Spurgeon, *Spurgeon's Sermons*, "The Raven's Cry," vol. 12, 1866. Spurgeon delivered this sermon on Sunday evening, January 14, 1866, at the Metropolitan Tabernacle, Newington, CT.

of Scots to declare about the Scottish Reformer John Knox, "I fear the prayers of John Knox more than all the assembled armies of Europe." There is a great dignity given to the people of God because we have been invited to come before God and make our requests known to Him. Prayer, therefore, becomes a means of grace even for those who do not know the Lord, since we have been given the dignity of causality and the privilege of interceding for a lost world. This is why Paul declares, "Do not be anxious about anything, but in everything by prayer and supplication with thanksgiving let your requests be made known to God" (Phil. 4:6).

This brings us to the third insight of this parable. It reflects a beautiful phrase I first heard from Dr. Steve Seamands, professor emeritus of theology at Asbury Theological Seminary. He called the kind of prayer Jesus is pointing to "sacrificial intercession." But he means more than the obvious point that we sacrifice our time to spend in prayer. He actually means that we take into ourselves the brokenness of others as we pray for them. Through prayer, we are brought up into the very agony of God Himself, who waits for the world to recognize who He is. God wants us to share in His own pain and suffering over a world that has turned their hearts from Him. Sometimes we mistakenly segment ourselves off from God, causing us to say things like "we do our part, and God does His part." This underestimates what actually happens in prayer. God's part involves our part. Our part is integral to God's work. We actually become sharers in the sufferings of Christ Himself. Peter calls us to rejoice "insofar as you share Christ's sufferings" (1 Peter 4:13).

We must recapture yet another means of grace that is particularly associated with sacrificial intercession; namely, fasting. Fasting, as understood by the larger society, normally means missing one or more meals for the purpose of losing weight or maintaining healthy bodily rhythms between eating and digesting. There is nothing wrong with that, but it is not what is meant by biblical fasting. Biblical fasting is focused on deep, intercessory prayer that allows us to completely focus on a spiritual objective in our lives, or in the lives of others. Satan relies heavily upon distraction and half-heartedness in our prayers. Fasting is an expression of self-denial that beckons us into a deeper place of spiritual warfare that is focused and able to tear down strongholds. There was an incident in the life of Jesus where His disciples expressed dismay that they were not able to cast a demon out of a young man. When they were in private, the disciples asked Jesus, "Why could we not cast it out?" Jesus replied that "this kind cannot be driven out by anything but prayer and fasting" (Mark 9:28–29).[6]

Oswald Chambers, the famous holiness preacher and author of the classic devotional *My Utmost for His Highest*, once said, "Intercession means to 'fill up what is lacking in the afflictions of Christ' (Col. 1:24), and this is precisely why there are so few intercessors. . . . Intercession is putting yourself in God's place; it is having His mind and His perspective."[7] It is this kind of sacrificial intercession that brings us beyond mere empathy for those who are suffering to an actual means of grace for them as we open ourselves up as channels of God's grace in their lives. This is why Scripture calls us to "carry each other's burdens, and in this way, you will fulfill the law of Christ" (Gal. 6:2).

But our parable ends with a question. It is rare that a parable ends with a question. This parable ends with the rather haunting question from our Lord: "When the Son of Man comes, will he find faith on earth?" (Luke 18:8). It takes the whole parable and presses it right into our own lives and hearts. When Jesus comes back, will He find a

---

6. The ESV has the "and fasting" as an alternative reading of the text.

7. Oswald Chambers, "Intercessory Prayer," December 13, *My Utmost for His Highest*. See also May 4, "Vicarious Intercession," https://utmost .org/intercessory-prayer/.

prayerless church? When Jesus comes back, will He find that we were laying hold of the inheritance that is ours in and through the gospel? When Jesus returns, will He find a church in prayer or one that relies upon its own methods, its own solutions, and its own ingenuity? Alfred Lord Tennyson once said, "More things are wrought by prayer than this world ever dreamed of: wherefore, let thy voice rise like a fountain for me night and day."[8] Prayer is what opened the Red Sea, brought water from the rock in the wilderness, and brought manna from heaven. Prayer made the sun stand still, brought down fire on Elijah's sacrifice, and overthrew Sennacherib's mighty army. Prayer healed the sick and raised the dead. Prayer has brought comfort and salvation to millions. Will we seize upon this wonderful means of grace for our lives and for the world? Prayer, in the great mystery of the church, has been given to us by God to join Him in establishing His purposes, changing the world and giving glory unto Himself.

8. Alfred Tennyson, "The Passing of Arthur," *Idylls of the King*.

# Chapter Five

# The Lord's Prayer as a Means of Grace

SCRIPTURAL BACKGROUND:
MATTHEW 6:9–13; LUKE 11:1–4

In the last chapter we explored how deep, sustained, persistent prayer is a means of grace in our lives and to the world. But the Lord also gave the church a set prayer shared by the entire church known as the Lord's Prayer.[9] It is significant that Luke 11:1 begins with a request from the disciples to Jesus, "Lord, teach us to pray." It is a request for a shared prayer for the community of God's people. In response, Jesus gives us the Lord's Prayer. We should understand that our

---

9. In the Roman Catholic tradition, it is called the "Our Father" prayer and does not include the doxological ending: "for thine is the kingdom, the power and the glory, forever and ever, Amen."

prayer lives should include both desperate, particularized prayer, "Lord, give me justice against my adversary" (as seen in chapter 4), as well as the regular rhythm of daily prayer that reaches beyond any particular crisis and embraces the broader work of God in our lives and in the world.

Because the Lord's Prayer serves as a means of grace, it has appeared in catecheses or discipleship guides across the centuries. There are two reasons for this. First, it is because the moral framework of the Ten Commandments (especially as deepened in the Sermon on the Mount) compels us to prayer, which acknowledges our need for the enabling presence of God. Second, the Lord's Prayer is the paradigm for all prayer, including set liturgical prayers as well as the kind of spontaneous prayers we might pray that are known only to God. The Lord's Prayer gives us the basic grammar of all prayer.

The overall structure of the Lord's Prayer is similar to the Ten Commandments. Broadly speaking, the Ten Commandments are divided between our moral obligations to God (commandments 1–4) and our moral obligations to our neighbor (commandments 5–10). In the same way, the Lord's Prayer is made up of five main phrases or petitions. The first two are clearly related to our life before God and His work in the world. The latter three give us the proper orientation toward ourselves and our neighbors. This brief overview of the Lord's Prayer is designed to point out the significance of the five phrases and how they serve as a means of grace for our entire life of prayer.

Just as the Ten Commandments are found in two locations in the Old Testament (Exodus 20 and Deuteronomy 5), the Lord's Prayer is found in two locations in the New Testament. It is found in Matthew 6:9–13 as a part of the Sermon on the Mount (Matthew 5–7) and in Luke 11:2–4 as a part of Jesus' teaching on prayer. In Luke's gospel, the prayer is given to us in an abbreviated form. But in both versions the same five phrases or petitions are found. Here are the two prayers as they appear in Matthew and Luke:

| Matthew 6:9–13 | Luke 11:2–4 |
| --- | --- |
| Our Father in heaven, hallowed be your name, | Father, hallowed be your name, |
| Your kingdom come, your will be done | Your kingdom come. |
| On earth as it is in heaven. | |
| Give us this day our daily bread. | Give us each day our daily bread. |

| | |
|---|---|
| Forgive us our debts, as we also have forgiven our debtors. | Forgive us our sins, for we ourselves forgive everyone who is indebted to us. |
| And lead us not into temptation, but deliver us from evil. | And lead us not into temptation. |

A brief examination of the overall structure reveals that the first two phrases focus on God and His name, His kingdom, and His will. The final three phrases focus on our bread, our sins, and our temptations. Even this most basic observation has the potential to dramatically change our prayer lives. If we think of our prayers, especially our more informal, spontaneous prayers, they almost always focus on our needs and the challenges we have with those around us. If we have time, we might pray about and think about God and His name, glory, will, and kingdom. Thus, from the outset, the Lord's Prayer calls for a radical reorientation of our prayer lives, putting God's glory and will before our needs.

You may also notice that when the Lord's Prayer is publicly prayed in church, it often includes the final phrase: "For yours is the kingdom, and the power and the glory forever, Amen." This final phrase is not found in the original teachings of Jesus but was liturgically added by the early church to assist the church in seeing the kingdom framework of the entire prayer. Since it is not always possible week after week to point out to congregations the kingdom orientation of the overall prayer, it was probably wise that this phrase was added to the prayer when it was prayed publicly. However, this guide will only focus on each of the five phrases found in the original teachings of Jesus.

## Petition #1: Our Father in Heaven, Hallowed be Your Name

### Our Father

At the very threshold of the Lord's Prayer we find a glorious revelation unmatched in the religious history of the world and known to us only by divine self-disclosure. The two words "our Father" usher us into a vibrant *relationship* with God. We pray not as slaves seeking to hear and obey a powerful master but as children who have been graciously ushered into the joyous presence of their father. We come not as lone and isolated searchers after God but as a part of the great communion of the saints. It is not my Master, or even my Father, but *our* Father. We are brought into the joyful presence of both the Trinity (of which Jesus and the Spirit also join in by saying "our Father") and the company of the redeemed. We should not miss the fact that the phrase "our Father" simultaneously implies both the doctrine of the Trinity and the doctrine of the communion of the saints. As the people of God, we are brought up into the fellowship, which heretofore has only been enjoyed in the mysteries of God's own triune life.

## *In Heaven*

We pray from the limited frame and perspective of earthbound space and time. However, God dwells in heaven. He is outside of time and sees the end from the beginning. When we pray, we enter into His presence knowing that we are thereby entering into His perspective and lordship over all of time and history. He is on the throne of the universe; we are not. This phrase reminds us that we are submitting our perspective to His perfect wisdom right at the outset of our prayer. So often what we call "unanswered prayers" have actually been answered from the perspective of heaven, but we have failed to discern the answer because it came to us in an unexpected way or will yet unfold in God's time, which is ever-present to Him.

## Hallowed Be Your Name

In the Scriptures, to call upon someone's name is to call upon the character of that name and the associated power identified with it. So, when we say, "Our Father, who art in heaven, hallowed be your name," we are acknowledging the holiness and the sacredness of His name. The Bible gives God many names. However, all of those names are summarized by the one title: holy. The word *hallowed* means "holy." It is not that there is a hierarchy of names, with ones like "Lion of the Tribe of Judah" and "Judge" near the bottom, and names like "Lamb of God" and "Savior" a bit higher, and finally, "Holy" at the top. God's character qualities cannot be ranked like that, because He bears all of them in their perfected state and in perfect harmony with all the others. Rather, the name "Holy" should be seen as containing *all* of God's other qualities and characteristics within the one affirmation. Thus, when we pray "Holy is your name," we are, in that one phrase, confessing all of God's nature and character in the single word! Interestingly, of all the names and titles attributed to God, only "holy" appears in triplicate form. It is known as the Trisagion (meaning triple holy) and appears in this form three times in the Bible. It first appears in Isaiah 6 when the prophet has his vision of heaven and sees the six-winged seraphs flying around the throne and crying out day and night, "Holy, holy, holy" (Isa. 6:3). It appears a second time in Psalm 99 where it serves as a refrain and appears three times: "Holy is he!" The threefold holy appears a third time in John's vision of heaven in Revelation. He also sees "six winged creatures" who cry out day and night, "Holy, holy, holy" (Rev. 4:8).

It is significant that both the Ten Commandments and the Lord's Prayer have this wonderful convergence in protecting and honoring the holiness of God's name. This is the foundation for all prayer and, indeed, our entire relationship with God. When Moses first encountered God at the burning bush, he was told to take off his shoes for he was on holy ground (Ex. 3:5). Likewise, when we first learn to pray and come into God's presence, we begin by recognizing that we are on holy ground. At the end of the ages when we gather round His throne, we will declare the holiness of God. All our prayers and our hopes and even our darkest pain must ultimately pass through the sanctifying fires of His holiness.

# Petition #2: Your Kingdom Come, Your Will Be Done on Earth as It Is in Heaven

## *Your Kingdom Come*

When we think about the word *kingdom*, our mind quickly goes to faraway images associated more with medieval Europe than with the world in which we live. Therefore, it is important at the outset to understand what the word *kingdom* means. It does not primarily refer to a geographical place the way we think of the word *kingdom*, such as the United Kingdom or the Kingdom of Saudi Arabia. It also should not be understood to refer to any particular political party or political plan. In the Bible, the kingdom of God is more about God's reign than a particular geographic realm or political plan. The kingdom of God is about God's kingly reign. God is the King. He rules and reigns over all.

When Jesus teaches us to pray that God's kingdom would come, it is a prayer that the rule of God would be fully known and established in the church, in our lives, and throughout the world. This kingdom transcends every country or political system because it sits in judgment over them all and, in the end, will triumph over them all. In the book of Revelation, Jesus is given the name King of kings and Lord of lords (19:16). This is the heart of the kingdom of God: Jesus Christ is Lord! To pray for God's kingdom to come is an acknowledgment that the rule and reign of God is coming, and so we are praying for the hastening of that day and that we would be fully in harmony with God's reign as it is breaking into the present order.

## *Your Will Be Done on Earth as It Is in Heaven*

There is a great gulf between the rule and reign of God in heaven and the rule and reign of God on earth. In heaven, God's rule and reign is fully known and acknowledged. In heaven there is no sin, injustice, or any deviation from God's glorious rule and reign. On earth, God's rule is only seen in distorted, fragmented ways. When we pray for God's will to be done on earth as it is in heaven, we are longing for the day when the reality of God's rule (which is already present in heaven) would fully manifest itself in the earth. In the incarnation of God in Jesus Christ, we were able to see up close the rule and reign of God fully present in Him. In Jesus Christ, the rule of God was inaugurated into the world in a fresh way. The first words of Jesus in His public ministry were, "The time has come. . . . The kingdom of God has come near. Repent and believe the good news!" (Mark 1:15 NIV). It is the announcement of the great invasion of God's rule into the broken, fallen world of sin and death. God's rule reverses the power of sin and overturns death itself. All through the ministry of Jesus we hear Him speaking of the kingdom of God, declaring, in word and deed, that the in-breaking of God's rule has finally begun.

Every gathering of believers around the world should be seen as a little outpost of the kingdom of God. The church is to be the living example of God's rule and reign in the world. The kingdom of God is, therefore, being dynamically revealed in history as His reign and rule extends through the preaching of the gospel and the empowerment of the Holy Spirit. In the church and in the lives of Christians we should see the realities of heaven made fully manifest. The world may be full of deceit and greed, but it should never be so in the church. The world may be full of evil and injustice, but it should never be so in the church. This is why it is so embarrassing when scandals break out in the church or in the lives of Christians. It discredits the very foundation upon which the church stands; namely, that it is an outpost of the rule and reign of God. This is also why it is so important for such scandals, when they do occur, to be swiftly acknowledged and repented of, lest "the Name of God is blasphemed among the Gentiles because of you" (Rom. 2:24).

This is why we daily pray that God's rule and reign would come and that the gap between His rule in heaven and His rule on earth would become narrower. When we fight for justice, we help narrow the gap. When we stand against evil, we help narrow the gap. This process continues until Jesus comes and fully consummates His kingdom, judges the world, defeats all demonic powers, vindicates His children, and fully ushers in the new creation, where God's rule and reign is without end. We do not know the exact process through which God's rule and reign will finally be fully established. We only know that the last enemy of God that will be destroyed will be death itself: "For he must reign until he has put all his enemies under his feet. The last enemy to be destroyed is death" (1 Cor. 15:25–26).

## Petition #3

### *Give Us Today Our Daily Bread*

This is the point in the Lord's Prayer when we transition from our prayers related to God's holiness, His will, and His kingdom to our own needs. There is nothing wrong with a prayer that contains the word *give* but we should not *start* our prayers this way. Before we ask God to give us something, we must first orient ourselves to Him and His rule and reign. This is why the Lord's Prayer is the model prayer. The Scriptures say, "Enter his gates with thanksgiving, and his courts with praise!" (Ps. 100:4). It does not say enter to His presence with petitions and His courts with requests. However, once we properly align ourselves to His rule and reign, then we are invited to ask God to meet our specific needs.

As a model prayer, the phrase "our daily bread" has two important features, which we should recognize. First, the word *bread* as it is used in this prayer is a word that symbolizes all of our basic needs. In ancient Israel, as in many parts of the world even today, bread was the staple of life. If Jesus' ministry had been in South India or in China, He might have said, "Give us our daily bowl of rice." The point is that it represents our daily needs. By extension, the phrase reaches beyond food to include everything we need for daily life, including food, clothing, housing, honest government, health, family, and friends, to name just a few.

The second, and equally important, feature of the phrase "our daily bread" is the force that lies behind the word *daily*. Notice that when God promises to meet our needs, it is a *daily* promise. In the days of the wilderness wanderings, the manna was provided daily. No manna was to be hoarded for future weeks (Ex. 16:13–33). It is an early example of God teaching His people about daily dependence upon Him. While the word *bread* encompasses everything we need in this life, it does not always come in advance installments. Many of us have sufficient provisions for our lives for months, or even years, in advance. This is a great blessing from God, but it can lead us to a lower awareness of our daily dependence upon God for everything we need.

The Scriptures give us a picture of two people with barns that are filled. The first picture is the righteous man of Psalm 144 (NIV). He has a barn "filled with every kind of provision." The picture is one of abundance. His "sheep will increase by thousands" (v. 13). His "oxen will draw heavy loads" (v. 14). How blessed is the one "of whom this is true" (v. 15). The second picture is the rich fool of Luke 12. His barns are also full of grain and goods. He has such an abundant crop that he has no place to store all of his grain. So, he decides to tear down his barns and build bigger ones. He then says to himself, "You have ample goods laid up for many years; relax, eat, drink, be merry" (12:19). But, unlike the righteous man of Psalm 144, this man is called a "fool" by God because he didn't realize that God was the source of his life. In fact, he did not realize that on that very night he was going to die (Luke 12:16–21). These two pictures reveal the importance of trusting God daily for our provisions and being generous with what we have. It may very well be that our abundance may be today's daily source for us as well as our neighbor in need.

## Petition #4: Forgive Us Our Debts as We Also Have Forgiven Our Debtors

### Forgive Us Our Debts

The fourth petition of the Lord's Prayer acknowledges that we stand as sinners before God and are in need of His forgiveness.[10] Sin refers to anything that contradicts, or is inconsistent with, God's holiness and thereby creates a breach in the relationship between ourselves and God. The Scriptures teach that sin is far more than merely the mistakes we make or even our violations of the Ten Commandments. Sin is the breaking of a divine *relationship*. The Scriptures also teach that there is no one

---

10. Some Christian traditions use the word *trespasses* whereas others use *debts*. Both words are used to speak about the weight of sin that is upon us.

without sin. This is taught in both the Old and the New Testaments. For example, in 1 Kings 8 we have Solomon's prayer of dedication for the temple. In the prayer, Solomon makes nine references to our sin, including the phrase "for there is no one who does not sin" (v. 46). Likewise, the New Testament teaches that "all have sinned and fall short of the glory of God" (Rom. 3:23). Because sin is not merely a matter of outward actions but a matter of the disposition of our hearts, then there is no one who is without sin. Therefore, the entire human race stands in a broken relationship with God. There are no exceptions. To make matters worse, there is nothing we can do to restore the relationship since we are so thoroughly oriented to resist God's will. It is a debt we cannot pay. In fact, Paul says that we are "dead in our trespasses and sins" (Eph. 2:1, 5; Col. 2:13). Dead people are powerless to help themselves. No amount of good works can heal the breach.

Hindus travel hundreds of miles to dip in the Ganges River, but it has no power to heal this relationship. Muslims pray every day, fast for a month each year, and even make a pilgrimage to Mecca, but none of these things have the power to take away sins. God alone must act on our behalf. The good news of the gospel is that this is precisely what

God has done by sending His Son into the world to die on the cross for our sins. In the Lord's Prayer, we ask God to forgive us our debts because it is something only He can do. We ask not on the basis of anything we have done, but by casting ourselves on God's mercy and trusting in the provision which has been made for us in Jesus Christ. Forgiveness is not offered to us because God just wants to forgive or feels compassion for us; it is very costly to God, as the penalty for that sin had to be paid for.

Paul says, "And you, who were dead in your trespasses and the uncircumcision of your flesh, God made alive together with him, having forgiven us all our trespasses, by canceling the record of debt that stood against us with its legal demands. This he set aside, nailing it to the cross" (Col. 2:13–14). This is our justification. But asking God to forgive us is also an ongoing, daily rhythm in our lives as we increasingly become aware of the great gulf between His holiness and our sinfulness.

## As We Also Have Forgiven Our Debtors

This part of the petition brings two very important truths to light. First, we see that the good news of the gospel is not an expression of cheap grace. In other words, God's forgiveness is not merely granted in isolation from the larger network of our relationships and our own grateful response to God's grace. We are saved and ushered into the community of God's redeemed people. We cannot and should not pretend that this is not so. Therefore, God's forgiveness is linked to our forgiving those who have sinned against us. In short, the vertical act of God's forgiveness in the Lord's Prayer is dynamically linked to the horizontal act of forgiving others. This teaching is so radical and so disturbing to our way of living and thinking that Jesus reinforced and restated this immediately after He taught His disciples the Lord's Prayer. The Lord's Prayer is found in Matthew 6:9–13 and is immediately followed with this teaching: "For if you forgive others their trespasses, your heavenly Father will also forgive you, but if you do not forgive others their trespasses, neither will your Father forgive your trespasses" (Matt. 6:14–15; see also Matt. 18:15–35). God's plan is not merely to reconcile people to Himself but to reconcile the whole human race to one another. Paul says, "If anyone is in Christ, he is a new creation. The old has passed away; behold, the new has come. All this is from God, who through Christ reconciled us to himself and gave us the ministry of reconciliation" (2 Cor. 5:17–18).

We are reconciled that we might become ministers of reconciliation. We know that we have truly heard and received the good news of God's forgiveness when we respond by forgiving others. Likewise, if we refuse to forgive those who have hurt us in some way, then we must not have ever really received the good news of God's grace, and we remain unreconciled to God. In short, God will not be reconciled to us if we refuse to be reconciled to our neighbor.

The second truth, which is related to the first, is the use of the word *we*. This reinforces the point that we should not overly privatize this prayer or, for that matter, the Christian faith as a whole. It is true that, through faith, we are personally reconciled to God. However, the gospel is never content to remain purely a private affair, or just a matter of our own heart before God. It may be never less than that, but it is certainly a great deal more than that. The Lord's Prayer points us to the deeper realization that the work of reconciliation includes an ever-widening circle of people whom God is calling to Himself. We may be justified as individuals, but the work of sanctification inevitably brings us into community, and, in the end, our final glorification occurs as joyful members of the body and bride of Christ.

# Petition #5: And Lead Us Not into Temptation, but Deliver Us from the Evil One

The fifth and final petition of the Lord's Prayer recalls the great cosmic battle of which we are a part. The true nature of this conflict is only slowly revealed in the Scripture. Beginning in the early part of the Old Testament, known as the Pentateuch (Genesis–Deuteronomy), God revealed to us that there were two paths, the way of blessing and the way of curse; the way of life and the way of death. We were called to choose which path we would follow (Deut. 27:14–26; 28:1–68; 30:19–20). In the Psalms, we are shown that there are two ways: the way of the righteous and the way of the wicked. This structure and tension is embedded into almost all of the Psalms but is best exemplified by Psalm 1, which pictures the righteous like a tree planted by streams of water and the wicked like the chaff that the wind blows away. In the book of Proverbs this tension is expressed in terms of the wise and the foolish. This is also a theme that dominates the whole of Proverbs and is perhaps best stated in the very first chapter, which portrays the wise as the one who fears God and the foolish as one who despises wisdom and shuns discipline (1:7). In the Old Testament, the prophets also describe these same two paths but use the language of the covenant to express it. There are those who obey God and keep the covenant and those who rebel against God and reject the covenant. The entire Old Testament lays the foundation for this massive struggle, which permeates the whole of life. There is the path of blessing, righteousness, wisdom, and obedience, and there is the path of curse, wickedness, foolishness, and rebellion.

Jesus reinforces this theme in the Sermon on the Mount when He speaks about two ways: the wide gate and the broad road that leads to destruction and the small gate and narrow road that leads to life. Many follow the former, but few find the latter (Matt. 7:13–14). However, it is in the Lord's Prayer that we fully recognize that this struggle is not only personal but also cosmic. It is not merely a struggle against evil but against the Evil One (i.e., the Devil or Satan). It is not merely a human struggle against "flesh and blood" but a struggle against "the cosmic powers" and the "spiritual forces of evil in the heavenly places" (Eph. 6:12). It is in the New Testament that we fully realize that behind all of the foolish, rebellious, wicked actions in the world stands Satan, who seeks to set up his own diabolical kingdom in contrast to the kingdom of God. It is in the New Testament that we see demons challenging the Son of God, not just the rebellious wicked world in opposition to Him. In the Lord's Prayer we pray that we might be delivered from the Evil One. In some translations, and frequently in churches when the Lord's Prayer is cited, it is stated as "deliver us from evil" rather than "deliver us from the Evil One." However, it is important to recognize that even when we say "evil," we must realize that Satan stands behind all of the evil in the world and that his pseudo-reign is far more than the aggregate accumulation of all the various acts of evil in the world.

It was important to start with the second phrase of this final petition to establish the larger context of evil. However, the first phrase raises a very important, if not troubling, question. Does God lead us into temptation? It is a question that does not have an easy answer. If He does lead us into temptation, then why does He do it? If He does not lead us into temptation, then why does He instruct us to pray that He wouldn't?

James teaches that "Let no one say when he is tempted, 'I am being tempted by God,' for God cannot be tempted by evil, and he himself tempts no one. But each person is tempted when he is lured and enticed by his own desire" (James 1:13–14). This clearly establishes the fact that God is not the tempter. Satan is the tempter, and we are also carried along by our own evil desires within us. However, it is important to remember that, unlike Zoroastrianism, Christianity does not believe in two equal cosmic powers, one good and one evil. Rather, the Bible affirms that God is sovereign over all, including the Evil One. This phrase of the Lord's Prayer is an acknowledgment of God's sovereignty over everything. Satan has been defeated by God at the cross, and the full ramifications of that victory are slowly unfolding according to God's time and God's plan. At the end of time, Satan will be cast into the lake of fire (Rev. 20:7–10), and God's triumph will be fully consummated and manifest for all to see. So, asking God to not "lead us into temptation" acknowledges God's ultimate sovereignty over all things. God is faithful in both walking with us through the fiery trials of life and, in other cases, delivering us from the fiery trial altogether. Why we are sometimes asked to walk through the dark valleys of pain, suffering, and temptation and, other times, we are powerfully protected from all of the same is a matter of the mystery of God's sovereign work and plan. When we do find ourselves in places of temptation or testing, it is good to remember that Jesus Himself was not exempt from being "led up by the Spirit into the wilderness to be tempted by the devil" (Matt. 4:1). The temptation was from the devil, but God may allow it if it serves His greater purposes in your life. This calls for humility and trust, which is certainly one of the great undergirding themes of all prayer, especially the Lord's Prayer.

## Amen

Although the text does not end with the word *amen*, this is such a widespread practice in prayers across the world, that it may be worth noting something about it. First of all, the word appears in both the Old and New Testaments and carries the meaning of "so be it" or "let it be so." It is used at the end of prayers (e.g., 1 Chron. 16:36; Eph. 3:20–21) as a final sign of God's sovereignty in our prayers. The etymology of the word *amen* is not certain. It is worth noting that the root of the Hebrew word for "amen" is the same as the word for "faith" (*āmēn/ʾāmán*). Thus, when we say "so be it," we are trusting God in faith, not simply acquiescing to fatalism. Furthermore, an ancient rabbinical teaching manual, known as the Talmud, says that the word is an acronym for the phrase "God is a trustworthy King." To say "amen" at the end of this or any other prayer is to acknowledge God's sovereignty and, in effect, to give God full and complete editing rights to your prayers. For example, you may be praying earnestly for God to give you a particular job you have applied for. God hears your prayer, but He knows that He has a better job waiting for you that you do not yet know about. So, you are praying, quite literally, "Lord, please give me this job," and after the "amen," God edits your prayer to say, "Lord, please do not give me this job." God answers the prayer, which we, at the moment, see as an unanswered prayer, but, later on, see as God's editorial work with fuller appreciation and gratitude. It was C. S. Lewis who first observed that, in prayer, we often ask for Band-Aids, when God knows we need major surgery. These are simple examples, but it does reveal something about the grand complexity of prayer when a finite being with limited knowledge and perspective is praying to the eternal Lord and God of the universe!

## Conclusion

We have examined each of the phrases of the Lord's Prayer. However, we began by stating that the Lord's Prayer is the model prayer for all prayer. It provides, as it were, the grammar for all prayer. Therefore, in conclusion, let's step back and take a sweeping look at the Lord's Prayer as a whole. It might be helpful to see the Lord's Prayer as a great drama of divine/human discourse that unfolds in three acts. Act One is the holiness and fatherhood of God. The whole prayer, as we observed, begins with an acknowledgment of God's holy name. Act Two, at the heart of the prayer, is the love of God. Here we meet the God who loves us, cares for us, and is prepared to meet our daily needs. Act Three is the sovereignty of God, the one in whom we must trust and rely upon, even in the face of what looks like unanswered prayer or situations that make us wonder if God is really in control. If we emphasize the love of God without the larger context of His holiness and His sovereignty, we end up drifting into mere sentimentality. If we emphasize holiness and sovereignty without the love of God, then we can all too easily drift toward a God who is powerful but aloof and distant. The Lord's Prayer provides the perfect frame of holiness, love, and sovereignty, a little mini-drama, which serves to enliven all of our prayers.

◆ Chapter Six ◆

# Reading Scripture as a Means of Grace

SCRIPTURAL BACKGROUND: NEHEMIAH 8:1–8

One of the abiding values of God's Word is that we are privileged to see the true people of God being the people of God in a wide variety of situations. We see them dancing on the shores of the Red Sea with tambourines in their hands: "I will sing to the LORD for he has triumphed gloriously; the horse and his rider he has thrown into the sea" (Ex. 15:1). We see them standing after three days of consecration in holy fear and breathtaking awe in the presence of God as smoke, thunder, and lightning go up from Mt. Sinai. The earth itself trembled as God spoke the covenant. Who can forget that high and holy moment when the great prophet Isaiah sees the Lord, high and lifted up, His train filling the temple, the angels crying "holy, holy holy." "Whom shall I send, and who will go for us?" He says, "Here I am! Send me" (6:8). But, it is not just earthquakes on Mt. Sinai, corporate celebrations, or glorious temple visions where we encounter God's voice. The Word of God also shares with us intimate moments between God and His people as when God calls "Samuel, Samuel" in the middle of the night to a young boy who replies, "Here I am!" (1 Sam. 3).

We are also allowed to see the people of God in difficult times. The people of God have to be the people of God not only in the mighty days of Moses but also during the lean days of Eli when "the word of the LORD was rare" (1 Sam. 3:1). Every man or woman of God longs to live in those times when the glory of the Lord fills the temple, visions of six-winged seraphs fill our lives, and the certainty of God's Word reverberates around our very being. But, some are chosen to live in a time when the ark of the covenant has been captured by the Philistines, a woman names her child Ichabod because the glory of the Lord has departed from Israel, and everyone does what is right in their own eyes. Some live in the days of Solomon when the temple was the splendor of the world and a wise king sat on the throne. Some, like Jeremiah, were called to be faithful to God even as they sat and wept on a hill overlooking the city of Jerusalem being burned to the ground and cried out "Daughter Jerusalem . . . your wound is as deep as the sea" (Lam. 2:13 NIV). We love to live in the exclamation marks of life, but sometimes we're called to be faithful in the question marks of life. The exclamation mark is sure and straight and the message is clear. A question mark is crooked and twisted and sometimes it's hard to see around it. Sometimes we don't know how to interpret the times we are in. We all know what it is like to look out on what we think are the promises of God as we hear some declare, "Wow, a land flowing with milk and honey" while others say, "Oh no, look at those giants!" (see Num. 13:27–28).

We must learn to recognize the times we live in. We are living in one of the great seams of history—the seam between modernity and post-modernity; Christendom and post-Christendom; and between a predominately Western Christianity and the emergence of a vibrant post-Western Christianity. We live in a post-Communist, post-Christendom, post-denominational, post-Western, post-Enlightenment, post-truth, and post-modern world. We don't even know what to call this new epoch we are entering . . . we just know we are "post" everything we have known. The point is that we live in a time of uncertainty, instability, and cultural and ecclesial chaos.

For many, many years, seminaries across North America prepared men and women for ministry in a society that was conceptualized as the modern-day equivalent of the promised land, a land full of spiritual milk and honey. Our nation was filled with steepled towns that rang their church bells as the faithful gathered to hear God's Word. We lived in a society where Judeo-Christian ethics were widely embraced by society at large. At some point, those of us who teach students, and those who pastor churches, slowly began to realize that we were no longer in the promised land but in something more akin to Babylonian exile. We had been preparing students to sing the songs of Zion, but they were sending texts and e-mails back to us saying that their days were filled with hanging their harps up and singing laments. I'm actually not lamenting that we are in a time of lament. Lament is good because lament is the mother of hope. Lament stimulates our collective memory as the people of God. We remember what once was and what could someday be again. The Psalms are full of this. What we don't want to do is to pretend that the landscape has not changed and fail to recognize the signs of our times.

Our text from Nehemiah reminds us that he lived at a seam time too. Nehemiah lived after the time of the exile, and yet the Messiah had not yet come. It was an in-between time. The long night of exile was over; Jews were returning, but there was still no Messiah. The walls of Jerusalem were torn down, and its gates were burned with fire. Hope seemed dim. This is when some of the great laments of the Psalms were written. Most Jews believed that their best days were behind them. We can only imagine the conversations that took place around the dinner table. It was a time of rebuilding and seeking to rekindle hope.

We don't know what kind of books might have been published in Nehemiah's day. If on the eighth day God had said, "Let there be Zondervan" or "Let there be Seedbed," just think of the books that could have been published. Moses could have been a best-selling author of *How to Pass through Your Red Sea* with his follow-up book, *The Purpose-Driven Nation.* Naturally, it would come with a study guide. Moses actually left us with five books. Nehemiah gave us a book too. We just call it Nehemiah, but if it were sold as a separate book, it might appear under the title *Living as a Jew in a Post-Judaism World* or *Life amidst the Rubble.* Because in this book, Nehemiah helps us understand what it means to be faithful to the call of

God in a post-Jewish, post-covenant, post-temple world, as well as our own post-Christendom, post-modern, post-denominational, post-truth world.

Nehemiah, as much as any of our dear brothers and sisters of the earlier covenant, would understand the world we inhabit. We have our Sanballats and Tobiahs—they are just known by different names, like Richard Dawkins and Sam Harris,[11] or sometimes they are pastors and bishops. We live at a time when the whole matrix of the educational system, the political apparatus, the media, entertainment, etc. all stand arrayed against the church and the Christian gospel. Many of you might even attend churches where your fellow members do not know God's Word. Nehemiah also lived in a world where the people of God did not remember their own Scriptures. They had forgotten the mighty acts of God. The Old Testament scholar Walter Brueggemann once said that the chief function of a prophet is to call people to remember, to remember the mighty acts of God. Nehemiah understood that.

We mainly remember Nehemiah as the one who rebuilt the walls of Jerusalem, but chapter 8 of our text

---

11. These are the names of two of the most prominent atheists in our day who have dedicated their lives to debunking Christian faith and identity.

tells us about something else he rebuilt. He rebuilt the pulpit. The pulpit, not just the temple and the walls, had become part of the rubble. Nehemiah had a great pulpit built. It is here in the midst of the rubble that we rediscover the power of reading Scripture as a means of grace. In Nehemiah 8:4 we are told that Ezra stood on "a wooden platform that they had made for the purpose." Ezra, the great priest of God, was called upon to deliver the word of God in uncertain times. He opened the Word of God and began to publicly read Scripture. This is the means of grace we are highlighting in this chapter. In Wesley's sermon on the means of grace (#16 in the standard collection), he lists this as the second means of grace—between prayer and the Eucharist. Nehemiah the governor and Ezra the priest appointed thirteen Levites to instruct the people in the Law while it was being read. We don't find a list of megachurch pastors or any fifth-century BC version of Christian celebrities or famous platform speakers. These are not household names, then or now. We find a list of Levites whose names you have never heard of: Jeshua, Bani, Sherebiah, Jamin, Akkub, Shabbethai, Hodiah, Maaseiah, Kelita, Azariah, Jozabad, Hanan, and Pelaiah. You may not have heard of any of them, but God put their names in the Bible. Verse 8 says that "they read from the book, from the Law of God, clearly, and they gave the sense, so that the people understood the reading."

The Word of God was publicly read and publicly heard. There is a unique power to hearing God's Word and hearing it declared with power. Probably the great saving grace of so many churches is that even when the gospel is not proclaimed from the pulpit, they still publicly read Scripture. We also live in a post-Gutenberg world, where the printing press has enabled most Christians to own a Bible. This is a blessing to the church, but from the time of the eighteenth-century and continuing to the present, the Word of God is overwhelmingly encountered silently as we read Scripture. Evangelicals often herald this as our daily "quiet time." But, in the process, our ears are not engaged, even if our mind is. Wesley taught us that there is a unique grace in hearing God's Word publicly with our ears. Most Christians, certainly most Methodists, know the powerful story of Wesley's conversion at Aldersgate on May 24, 1738, when his heart was strangely warmed. What you may not know, is that it was a Moravian layperson, a painter by trade, named William Holland who read Luther's preface to the book of Romans that night. Holland had himself just been gloriously converted and transformed by hearing

Luther's preface to the Galatians read by Charles Wesley on May 17, just one week earlier. Charles Wesley was sick in bed and read it from a weakened state, and his own life was transformed. There is a power in hearing God's Word read. Paul said, "Faith comes from hearing, and hearing through the word of Christ" (Rom. 10:17).

The most sacred spot on the campus of Asbury Theological Seminary is Estes Chapel. It is there that the Word of God is read and proclaimed multiple times every week at the seminary. More than one million of our one-hundred-million-dollar comprehensive campaign was designated for renovating Estes Chapel. It involved a year of work, culminating in the rededication of the space on May 8, 2018. We decided to precede the dedication with a public reading of Scripture in Estes Chapel. During the weeks leading up to the rededication, we had the entire Bible publicly read in Estes Chapel in shifts, filled mostly by students, which continued morning and night. It was done as a sign of the importance of the public reading of Scripture as a means of grace. It was also done as a prophetic reminder to the church at large of our commitment to the power of God's Word. The mission of Asbury Seminary is to "prepare theologically educated, sancti-fied, Spirit-filled men and women to evangelize and to spread scriptural holiness throughout the world." The phrase "spread scriptural holiness" is our way of declaring our mission to proclaim God's Word to the ends of the earth. Asbury remains committed to give to the world a whole new generation of Banis and Sherebiahs and Jamins and Hodiahs and Kelitas and Azariahs! This is the need of the hour—men and women called to faithfully teach people the Word of God in the midst of the rubble. We are committed to boldly proclaim the Word of God in the face of unbelief. Pastors throughout the United States and the world must remain true to God's Word even if their friends and colleagues in the clergy itself become cynical. We are the inheritors of the true gospel, not a domesticated, truncated, sub-Christian one that masquerades as the real thing. The great project of this new generation of Christians is the recovery of the glorious gospel and the full recognition that the Word of God is still God's great bulwark of righteousness that stands against and exposes the wicked designs of this world.

According to Nehemiah 4:17–18, they rebuilt the walls of Jerusalem with a trowel in one hand and a sword in the other. They understood the times they lived in. If you had gone around the broken walls of Jerusalem, every one of them would have preferred to live their lives with a tambourine in their hand, but instead they were called to live with a trowel and a sword. A time of rebuilding, a time of remembering, a time of hope.

We are living in amazing times. On the one hand, from a global perspective, the church of Jesus Christ is growing and flourishing unlike any time in human history. At the same time, mainline Protestantism in North America and Western Europe has been imploding at an alarming rate. We have to understand both of those dynamics. The center of gravity for the world Christian movement has shifted, and you may find yourself in a post-Christian West, even as many other parts of the world are experiencing the sunrise of a vibrant post-Western Christianity. We must recapture our commitment to the centrality of Jesus Christ and the power of God's Word. This is the day when, like Nehemiah of long ago, we must rebuild the pulpit and faithfully instruct the people of God in the Word of God. No pastor has the right to invent new doctrines. The job of any pastor is not to invent doctrine but to uphold the faith once and for all delivered to the saints (Jude 1:3). The post-Christian culture will pressure the church in a thousand ways to abandon the gospel and compromise the Word of God. Every voice will cry out to the church to measure its success by worldly standards. What is the size of your church? How much money does the pastor get paid? How nice is the parsonage? What kind of pension plan do we have? Is your church popular? Such questions must be regarded as distracting arrows from the pit of hell.

Some pastors will be called by God to lead charges with responsibility over thousands of members. For others, faithfulness means feeding a small flock and defending a relatively remote outpost of the kingdom. But never forget that whatever act we faithfully do in God's name, the whole incarnation is present in seed form. When Jesus touched the leper, it wasn't just a stepping stone to the cross. The whole cross was always in seed form in everything Jesus did. There are no stepping stones to the kingdom. There is no denominational ladder to climb. There is no career path stretching out in front of pastors. All Christians, especially pastors, are called to bear the cross of Jesus into the world.

The Word of God is one of the most powerful means of grace God has given to His church. Take a moment to reflect on the power of God's Word. The Bible opens with God saying, "Let there be light." God spoke that word in the midst of chaos, and light dawned upon the world. That light shines to this very day. Jesus said, "Lazarus come forth" and not only was death reversed for Lazarus, but that word echoes down to every tomb and body of the faithful throughout all of history who, someday, will rise to resurrected life, and death will finally be vanquished. That great song that Paul gives us will be our song: "'Death is swallowed up in victory. O death, where is your victory? O death, where is your sting?' The sting of death is sin, and the power of sin is the law. But thanks be to God, who gives us the victory through our Lord Jesus Christ" (1 Cor. 15:54–57). Jesus said, "Go therefore and make disciples of all nations" (Matt. 28:19), and the whole church of Jesus Christ was born and now reaches to the ends of the earth! This is the power of God's Word in the world: sinners are redeemed, bodies are healed, forgiveness is received, and reconciliation is wrought. It is truly a powerful means of grace. We must learn to reinhabit the kind of robust, apostolic Christianity that is necessary to face the challenges of our day. We must rediscover vibrant confidence in the public preaching of the Word of God, public confidence in the supremacy of Christ and the ongoing power of the Christian gospel!

In 2012, it was the one hundredth anniversary of the sinking of the *Titanic*, which sank on April 15, 1912. There has been considerable speculation over the years among *Titanic* enthusiasts over what caused the mighty ship to sink on its maiden voyage. Some have argued that the tragic accident was caused by a faulty rudder. Others insisted that it was ultimately caused by poor communications or the angle at which Captain Edward Smith hit the iceberg that sent the mighty ship more than two miles beneath the surface of the ocean. However, a study of scientists has concluded that the best explanation for the disaster was something far more mundane: second-rate rivets.

In the book *What Really Sank the Titanic: New Forensic Discoveries*, Jennifer McCarty and Timothy Foecke argue that the vessel's manufacturer, Harland and Wolff, was under so much pressure to secure sufficient quantities of iron to make the rivets for the vessel that they made some crucial compromises.[12] The White Star Line company that built the *Titanic* was under competition from another company named Cunard in an age when the construction of luxury ocean travel by Belfast shipyard workers translated into child labor, exhausting work schedules to meet deadlines, and enormous pressure to cut corners. McCarty and Foecke argue that in the rush to get the *Titanic* afloat

---

12. Jennifer Hooper McCarty and Timothy Foecke, *What Really Sank the Titanic: New Forensic Discoveries* (New York, NY: Citadel Press Books, 2008).

first, they ended up with an impressive looking vessel but one that was made with substandard materials. At the time of the *Titanic's* construction there was a shortage of quality iron. According to records, managers turned a deaf ear to numerous objections about the potential hazard of using substandard rivets. But everything was sacrificed to keep the *Titanic* on schedule.

Forty-nine rivets have now been recovered from the wreckage and a forensic analysis revealed that they, indeed, contained high levels of slag, making the iron brittle. These tests reveal that the rivets used in constructing the *Titanic* were, in fact, substandard and did not meet the design specifications. The *Titanic* could have struck an iceberg and stayed afloat even if as many as four of its sealed compartments were flooded. Instead, so many rivets popped along the starboard side of the ship that five of the sixteen compartments ended up flooding, sending more than 1,500 people to their deaths.

This story is a powerful reminder of the importance of not forgetting the basic fundamentals when building a big project. In the scale and grandeur of a project like the *Titanic* with hardwood dance floors, hanging chandeliers, and solid brass faucets, it was all too easy to not think about the importance of a lowly rivet. All too often we think that building a successful ministry is something akin to our version of hardwood dance floors, beautiful chandeliers, and solid brass faucets.

But actually, effective ministry is about rivets: the Word of God, the power of prayer, the anointing of the Spirit, the supremacy of Christ, the church as the embodiment of the new creation, and the compelling truth and power of the gospel for a broken world. These are the rivets you need. Because it is through them that God transforms the nations and summons the world to Himself. What an amazing means of grace God's Word is.

# Chapter Seven

# Works of Mercy as a Means of Grace

SCRIPTURAL BACKGROUND: MATTHEW 25:31–46;
1 CORINTHIANS 11:23–32

Many churches follow the basic rhythms of the church year. The purpose of the church year is to collectively disciple the church into a way of living and thinking that reflects the grand, redemptive work of the triune God in the world. It forces us to not cherry-pick the gospel but to walk through all of it. Although we are not dedicating a chapter to the theme, it should be noted that the church year is itself a means of grace to us. In a sense, by following the church year, the church corporately reenacts the great redemptive themes of God's work beginning with God the Father revealing His purposes in the prophets of the older covenant as we await the coming Messiah (Advent), to the the incarnation of God the Son through the birth of Jesus (Christmas and Christmastide), His public ministry (Epiphany), His passion (Lent), His resurrection (Easter), His ascension (Ascension Sunday), and the coming of the Holy Spirit, the third person of the Trinity (Pentecost).

Each season of the church year comes with its own unofficial liturgical symbols. Advent is a four-week season of waiting and expectation, and its most common liturgical symbol is the Advent wreath with the four candles. Each candle represents various aspects of our waiting and anticipation. If you go into a church and see an Advent wreath, you know it is Advent, don't you? Christmas is a twelve-day season symbolized by manger scenes, Chrismon/Christmas trees, many nativity reenactment plays, and so forth. If you walk into a church and see a Christmas tree or, better yet, a manger built on the stage with straw scattered about, you know it is Christmas. Epiphany is the most neglected season of the church year. The word *Epiphany* means "manifestation" and refers to the glorious light of the face of Christ revealed in public ministry from the baptism of Jesus all the way to His transfiguration. Its central symbol is the wise men who arrived a few years after the birth of Christ, but Epiphany's central symbol has become swallowed up by Christmas since we normally celebrate the coming of the wise men during Christmas. The central symbol of Lent is, of course, the cross, and this is also accompanied by passion plays. The central symbol of Easter is the empty tomb and sunrise services. The central symbol of Pentecost is a descending dove or, perhaps, fire, as we remember the Holy Spirit descending upon the church and empowering God's people with His presence for our shared mission. There are, of course, hymns written for each season, and many hymn books are organized both thematically and around the church year.

Later in this chapter I will reflect more on the central symbols of Lent—the cross, the towel and basin, and the broken bread—in light of the overall theme of this book: the means of grace. But we will begin by looking at a whole new category of the means of grace, which we have not yet discussed. It is here that John Wesley helps us in an enormous way as we think about the means of grace. Wesley took the key insights of sixteenth-century Reformation theology and expanded them to embrace a more holistic and fully biblically integrated vision. The idea of the means of grace did not originate with Wesley. In fact, it was a well-established theology among the Puritans in the sixteenth century, Anglicans in the seventeenth century, and before that in both Lutheran and Roman Catholic teaching. However, Wesley expanded the idea with a very important distinction, which is the theme of this chapter.

Within the larger frame of the means of grace, Wesley makes a distinction between what he calls "works of piety" and "works of mercy." For Wesley, works of piety refer to all the means of grace we have explored so far in this book: prayer, reading Scripture, baptism, receiving the Eucharist, and so forth. It is all the ways God works with us to conform us to the image of Christ. Most of us, by default, tend to equate the means of grace with what Wesley calls works of piety. But works of piety constitute only half of a Wesleyan understanding of the means of grace. The other half is known as works of mercy. Christians who belong to the Wesleyan stream sometimes refer to the "second half of the gospel" in reference to sanctification, which stands alongside justification, the "first half of the gospel." In the same way, I would like to suggest that we refer to the "second half of the means of grace" as works of mercy. It is here that Wesley understood that our lives should be focused outward as a means of grace to a lost and broken world. For Wesley, works of mercy would include things like visiting the sick, going to prisons, feeding the hungry, fighting for justice and racial reconciliation, to name a few. We might say that this is the *missional* side of the means of grace. The first half is about loving God with your heart, soul, mind, and strength. The second half is about loving your neighbor as yourself. These works of mercy are not ancillary to Christian identity any more than sanctification is an elective aspect of the Christian view of salvation. The means of grace include both works of piety and works of mercy.

Wesley's profound insight into the means of grace blasts through many of the contemporary and tragic tensions between evangelical faith and works of justice. The divide between evangelism on one side and social justice on the other has left many Christians confused as they see them as two separate spheres. But, we are called to embody both of these and live fully in the vibrant embrace of both. Historically, we need to remind ourselves and the world that Christians were on the forefront of issues like the abolition movement of the eighteenth century, child labor laws and women's suffrage in the nineteenth century, and civil rights in the twentieth century. Christians around the world have built countless hospitals, schools, and orphanages to alleviate human suffering. Ministries like the Red Cross, Alcoholics Anonymous, Bread for the World, World Relief, World Vision, Samaritan's Purse, International Justice Mission, and hundreds of others were all started by evangelical Christians. Bryan Stevenson, the founder of the Equal Justice Initiative, whose story has now been made into the film *Just Mercy,* says repeatedly that his faith is what informs all that he does. In fact, Christian churches provide more money and labor on behalf of the poor and disenfranchised than any other non-governmental group.

We do not accept the narrative that the only things evangelical Christians are interested in is the sweet bye-and-bye or, even worse, some truncated Christianity that reduces the whole gospel to a privatized faith in our hearts. In fact, we are working tirelessly on behalf of the poor, the disenfranchised, those unjustly sitting on death row, the immigrant, and so forth. Historically, evangelicals have always been deeply committed to social causes, and we should never permit the unbiblical divide between evange-lism and social action. The contemporary ambivalence has come largely because social action in the late nineteenth and twentieth centuries became distorted into what was called the "social gospel," which tended to minimize the cross and resurrection and downplay personal conversion. We rightly resisted that. But evangelicals should none-theless still be committed to addressing structural evils of society as well as alleviating personal suffering in every arena where it is found.

The challenge is to navigate the relationship between social action and evangelism well. Some evangelicals see social action as a *bridge* to evangelism. Others conceptualize social action as a natural *consequence* of evangelism. Still others try to see the two as complementary partners. In any case, they are broadly understood as vitally important but distinct ministries of the church. Evangelism is understood narrowly as an explicit presentation of the gospel, and social action is viewed as serving a supporting role, which bears witness to the gospel or, at times, a tool that leads to a greater acceptance of the gospel message. Sometimes social action is portrayed in ways that convey the idea that it is a form of stealth evangelism, or a strategic kind of tactic, that has no lasting merit unless it culminates in evangelism. Once evangelism and social action are conceptualized as two separate spheres, it is inevitable that evangelism is given a priority over social action and various explanations are required to demonstrate how social action leads to, or culminates in, or arises out of, evangelism and church-planting.

This is where Wesley's understanding of the means of grace captures the great theological point that you cannot love God with your heart, soul, mind, and strength unless you are also loving your neighbor as yourself. Jesus was asked for one great commandment, but He gave us two, and what God has joined together, we should not separate. This will finally all come together into one seamless, glorious truth in the last chapter in this book when we focus on love as the crowning means of grace: to be made perfect in love is to learn to seamlessly love God *and* your neighbor through the redirected heart, which is the truest testimony to sanctification.

We see this in Wesley's letter to Miss J. C. March in 1775. Wesley says to her, "Do you want to know how to dedicate your life to God? I will tell you how . . ." Wesley then points her (and us) out into the world: "Go and see the poor and sick in their own poor little hovels. Take up your cross" and bear it into the world. Wesley made this same point in his sermon "On Visiting the Sick." The sick for Wesley are not just those who are bodily sick but all those who have been wounded by the fall, believer and unbeliever alike, who need the grace of God. It is found repeatedly in Wesley's multiple expositions of Matthew 25: "Lord, when did we see you hungry, or thirsty, or a stranger needing clothes, or sick, or in prison, and did not help you?" Matthew 25:31–46 is the focal point of this mediation. It is here that we hear those remarkable words of Jesus, which should be before us at all times: To the righteous He says: "As you did it to one of the least of these my brothers, you did it to me" (v. 40). And to the wicked: "As you did not do it to one of the least of these, you did not do it to me" (v. 45). When Wesley insisted that faith must be operationalized, he was restoring biblical Christianity! Let us not miss the powerful message of Matthew 25. Brothers and sisters, it is Jesus who stands as the poor at our doorsteps and is hungry. It is Jesus who weeps as the immigrant at our borders and feels abandoned as a child in those detention centers. It is Jesus who sleeps in the homeless shelters and stands cold and poorly clothed in our streets. It is Jesus who languishes on death row. It is Jesus who groans over the pollution that has marred His creation. In today's world, it is vital that we recapture this historic theme in our biblically faithful witness.

For Wesley, the gospel is both sacramental and social. It is both personal and corporate. It embraces both personal conversion and working to see the kingdom manifest in the whole of society. The gospel engages our hearts and our hands. It is not just about becoming a Christian (justification) but also living as a transformed Christian (sanctification). The gospel is about our faith and our faithfulness and is embodied in both proclamation and social action. For Wesley, salvation was never less than justification by faith, but it was also about the necessity of good works!

Wesley sees this not only as our embodiment as the means of grace to the *world*, but in a remarkable way, precisely at the point where we embody the justice of God, the compassion of God, and the grace of God to those who do not deserve it, we find God's grace breaking into our own lives as we are shaped and formed in the process of serving. We do not accept the modern distinction between the "poor" and the "deserving poor," for this has all too often been used as an excuse to remain passive in the face of a world in need. Christ meets us, even in those whose lives are broken by decisions of their own making. Our responses may vary, but we cannot dismiss the face of Christ in the brokenness of all those who are poor and disenfranchised. We thank God for both the Billy Grahams and the Mother Teresas of the world, since both embody the in-breaking of the new creation into the present order.

The full meaning of the word *evangelism* is not just *believing* good news; it is the *embodiment* of the good news. The gospel is about nothing less than a radical reorientation of our life in the world. Paul was as committed to planting churches in his missionary journeys as he was to raising money to relieve the poor caught on the wrong end of the Jerusalem famine (1 Cor. 16:1–4; 2 Cor. 8:1–9:15; Gal. 2:10; and Rom. 15:25–29). This is why Wesley preached salvation by grace through faith to miners and bricklayers, as well as opposed slavery in his famous final letter to William Wilberforce written on February 24, 1791.

There are many ways we can serve the poor. It may be working in soup kitchens, helping in a homeless shelter, or providing clothing for the needy. Most correctional facilities have programs for inmates who need mentors, help in earning their GED (high school diploma equivalent), spiritual counseling, or help with substance abuse. Some facilities even have programs helping incarcerated fathers learn how to become better fathers for their children on the outside. Prisoners have always been of special concern for Methodists. Prisoners need help in everything from how to apply for jobs to how to manage their anger to how to develop their construction skills or discover skills that they do not know they have. Many communities have grandparents who face special needs in caring for their grandchildren because the parents of their grandchildren are in prison or have deserted their children. These are all examples of how we can connect with countless ministries revealing the heart of Jesus to a broken world.

It is here that we turn to our other text and those timeless words of Jesus, "This is my body given for you," which is symbolized in the Lord's Supper with the bread (1 Cor. 11:24). We have *under-heard* those words if we think about them as only those cherished words we hear at the Lord's Supper. For they are actually the defining words of the incarnation itself when Jesus says, "A body have you prepared for me" (Heb. 10:5). The incarnation is Jesus' self-donation or self-sacrifice of His body for the world. He did it while we were sinners (Rom. 5:8). Works of mercy are never merely tasks that we do. Rather, we are united with Jesus in a sacramental presence in the world through which our bodies represent Him or point to Him as we walk in the world.

God has given Himself completely and wholly to us. The incarnation and the cross both declare the powerful truth of God's self-donation to His creation. We should not shy away from the bloody, fleshly self-sacrifice of Jesus Christ on the cross on our behalf. It is more than just an act that enables our justification before God; it is also our participation with Jesus, the friend of sinners, the man of sorrows, in His redemptive work to reconcile all things to Himself. We are called to give ourselves to one another and to the world. "This is my body, broken for you" becomes the sign of our *sacramental presence* as the broken bread of Jesus to a hungry world. Our acts of mercy become daily gifts we give to the world to reflect the self-donation of God Himself. Scripture calls Christians to "present your bodies as a living sacrifice, holy and acceptable to God, which is your spiritual worship" (Rom. 12:1). Amazingly, our most spiritual act of worship is tied to the offering of our bodies as "living sacrifices." Tish Warren humorously records a sign she saw on the wall of a new monastic community that read, "Everyone wants a revolution. No one wants to do the dishes."[13] New Testament scholar N. T. Wright observed that at the Last Supper, Jesus did not give His disciples a theory of the atonement but a deed to be acted out with tangible, physical signs.

At the very least, the physical elements of bread and wine are tangible reminders of the physical reality of the incarnation and Jesus' real sacrifice of His body for the sins of the world. But they are also a reminder of the physicality of what it means for us to be His embodied ambassadors in the world. The privatization of our faith has left us with a truncated gospel, which seems increasingly unable to

---

13. Tish Harrison Warren, *Liturgy of the Ordinary* (Downers Grove, IL: IVP Books, 2016), 35.

address the most pressing issues of our day. We walk into the world every day as the *church*, those who are baptized, the embodied presence of the in-breaking new creation. Our missional acts of mercy in the world recognize the deeply spiritual and theological significance of our lives in the world. We are all indebted to Eastern Orthodox Christians for their emphasis on the missional nature of the sacraments. The Lord's Supper is not only God's bread for us, but it transforms us into bread for a hungry and needy world. When we come to the table, we are already mystically foreshadowing that great banquet of the age to come, the celebration that is the sign and seal of the new creation, and that must be made manifest through us to *this* creation!

In the contemporary church, we spend quite a bit of time and energy making our worship services relevant for the world, but have we forgotten the deeper call to make *ourselves* relevant to the world through our embodied transformation into the likeness of Christ? Christians have sometimes inadvertently portrayed salvation as an escape from time, rendering time meaningless, when the very core of the gospel is, through the incarnation, God's invasion into time and space to redeem it and transform the world.

So all the means of grace that we call "works of piety" are inextricably linked to all the means of grace that we call "works of mercy." The Lord's Supper is not simply a means of grace where our sins are forgiven (i.e., a work of piety), but it is also our being transformed to be God's broken bread for a world of suffering (i.e., a work of mercy). Reading Scripture is more than shaping us spiritually (i.e., a work of piety); it is also our proclamation as we proclaim the word of reconciliation to a lost world (i.e., a work of mercy). Prayer is not merely to calm our lives and form us (i.e., a work of piety); it is through prayer that we wage war on behalf of the lost and a broken world (i.e., a work of mercy). All the works of piety have a corresponding second half of the means of grace, which find their place in works of mercy. They are not two things but one thing, which we call, as a way of summary, the means of grace. May this devotional help us all to reflect deeply not just on our inner life before God but also on our own presence in the world. For, as we learn to walk with Jesus in the midst of a world of pain and brokenness, we see in fresh ways the face of God.

St. Teresa of Avila, the great sixteenth-century Spanish mystic and theologian and first woman to be named a doctor of the church, once wrote,

Christ has no body on earth but yours; no hands but
yours; no feet, but yours.

Yours are the eyes through which Christ's compassion for the world is to look out;

Yours are the feet with which he is going about
doing good;

and yours are the hands through which he blesses
the world.[14]

---

14. *The Life and Prayers of Saint Teresa of Avila* (Boston: Wyatt North Publishing, 2012), 64.

# Chapter Eight

# Worship as a Means of Grace

SCRIPTURAL BACKGROUND: ROMANS 12:1–2

Bob Mumford, a popular Bible teacher in the 1970s, once told the story of a dream he had. In the dream he saw his own familiar Bible lying open on the table where he had his morning devotions. However, in his dream, his Bible was very unusual. As he turned the pages, some of the pages were large and well-marked; others were very tiny, like little postage stamps in his Bible. He didn't even need to ask, as often happens in biblical revelation, "Lord, what does this mean?" because he instantly understood. It was the Lord showing him that he loved to preach on certain texts of Scripture while leaving so many others untouched, unread, and un-preached. He took it as a renewed call to preach the *whole* Word of God, not just his favorite texts. If the truth were told, we all probably need that dream in our lives.

One of the great values of reading and studying the entire Bible is that it gives us the ability to step back and look at even a very familiar passage of Scripture and see it within the larger context of the Bible as a whole.

This is certainly true of the Scripture focus for this chapter: Romans 12:1–2. It is one of the most familiar texts of Scripture in the New Testament. It would be one of the big pages in our dream. We love to quote it. It is definitely underlined in our Bibles or highlighted on our Kindles. But, perhaps we need to take a closer look at how this text fits into Paul's larger argument in the book of Romans.

## The Context of Paul's Epistle to the Romans

Whenever I read Paul's epistle to the Romans, I do so with a sense of awe at the expansive exposition of the gospel found here, as well as the impact of this epistle on our history as Christians.

Paul gives us an unmatched explanation of the gospel, which has been the source of countless renewals and spiritual awakenings in our history as Christians.

When Augustine heard those famous words *tolle lege, tolle lege* ("take up and read") in the year 386, it was to Romans 13:13–14 that he turned and was converted. In 1519, when Martin Luther was in the Black Cloister Tower, it was Romans 1:17, "the righteous shall live by faith," that changed Luther's life, and the world was never the same. Luther said when he understood Paul's meaning, "I felt like I was born again and entered paradise itself through open gates." The Methodists' story is intertwined with this book, as John Wesley went unwillingly down to that Moravian prayer meeting at Aldersgate on May 24, 1738, and heard that exposition from Romans that warmed his heart and changed the world. One of the great chapters in the Great Awakening opened on that night.[15] Karl Barth, the twentieth-century Swiss theologian, was in seminary being shaped by liberal theology when he turned one night to the book of Romans, and it rocked his world. He went through the whole epistle and wrote a fresh commentary on it. The publication of *Der Römerbrief* (The Epistle to the Romans) was famously described by Karl Adam, a

---

15. The Great Awakening refers to a series of revivals that took place between 1737 and 1740 and is associated with the preaching of John Wesley, Jonathan Edwards, and George Whitefield, among others.

reviewer, like "a bombshell dropped on the playground of the theologians." I could go on, for the list includes so many others from William Tyndale to N. T. Wright. This grand Christian vision has captivated Christians all through history.

The first few verses of Romans 12 serve as a kind of hinge between the two great sections of Romans chapters 1–11 and chapters 12–16. The first part of Romans focuses on what God has done for us in Jesus Christ, and the second section focuses on the implications of it for our lives as Christians. The first word in Romans 12 is the word *therefore*. There is a famous rule of thumb that states when you come upon the word *therefore* in the Bible, you should always ask the question, "What is the 'therefore' there for?"

So, let's explore that. As previously noted, Paul sets forth the magnificent theological vision of Christian identity in Romans 1–11. In these chapters we learn that all have sinned and fallen short of the glory of God (3:23). We read that there is none righteous, not even one (3:10). Jew and Gentile alike are under the bondage of sin and in need of God's grace (3:19). It is in these chapters that Paul declares that we are saved by grace through faith by way of the completed work of Jesus Christ on the cross. That's what the "therefore" is there for!

We learn in Romans 1–11 to embrace Abraham as our father in faith (4:16) who showed us what it meant to trust in God's Word even on Mt. Moriah with a knife in his hand and a promise in heart. The phrase "Abraham believed God, and it was credited to him as righteousness" (Rom. 4:3, 22) is one of the most important phrases in the passage. That's what the "therefore" is there for!

Romans teaches us that we were once in Adam, full participants in a race condemned for rebellion with no way out. But God, in His mercy, sent Jesus, and now there is a new head of a new redeemed community. We are no longer "in Adam" but "in Christ." Jesus Christ became the second Adam, inaugurating not the old creation under that first Adam but the new creation under this second Adam (5:12–17). Paul declares that "for as by the one man's disobedience the many were made sinners, so by the one man's [Jesus Christ's] obedience the many will be made righteous" (5:19). That's what the "therefore" is there for!

We have, through faith, been united with Him in His death so that we might also be united with Him in His resurrection. "We were buried therefore with him by baptism into death, in order that, just as Christ was raised from the dead by the glory of the Father, we too might walk in newness of life" (6:4). That's what the "therefore" is there for!

Jesus also came out of Egypt, recalling the whole history of Israel. Jesus has recapitulated the whole of creational and redemptive history in His own life. Paul demonstrates how Jesus fulfills all the hopes and promises of Israel. He became the new Moses (10:5–19) who led a new people—not only the blessed Jews but men and women from every tribe and tongue and people—to an even greater promised land. As the new Moses, He fulfilled all of the Law and He became a new Lawgiver, not abolishing the Law but fulfilling it and enabling us to live by the deeper Law not written on tablets of stone but on human hearts. The Law that produced death in us is now made alive again through the obedience of Jesus Christ! We are no longer slaves to sin but slaves of righteousness (6:15–23). That's what the "therefore" is there for!

Jesus became a new high priest. He is both priest and sacrifice. He is both the promise and the keeper of the promise. He is both the Lawgiver and the fulfillment of the Law. That's what the "therefore" is there for!

He was revealed as King, fulfilling Davidic promises, as great David's greater Son, one who would sit not on a mere earthly throne but at the right hand of God the

Father Almighty, as the resurrected Lord. As the risen Lord He sends us His Spirit, enabling us to be adopted as His sons and daughters that we might cry, "Abba! Father!" (8:15). That's what the "therefore" is there for!

He came as God's Suffering Servant, bearing all the lament of the world and the brokenness of a world hopelessly lost. He became the final sacrifice, not with the blood of bulls and goats but with the precious blood of the incarnate God-man, fully God and fully man (3:25; 5:9). God, like we never saw Him, and man like we never saw him. We may have captured glimpses of God at Mt. Sinai or His glory as it passed by, but now we see God face-to-face in the full glory of Jesus with a glory that unlike Moses' face was not fading but one that shines with an everlasting glory! But, not only do we see God in Jesus Christ, we see man in Jesus Christ. We see our full humanity, men and women, created in the image of God, now marred and bruised by the fall. The image of God, so gloriously revealed in Genesis, is never mentioned outside of Genesis again throughout the entire Old Testament. We re-meet the image of God as it explodes once again in the New Testament at the dawn of the new creation—Jesus Christ, the full and unmarred image of God walking in flesh amongst us. We are predestined to be conformed to the image of His Son (8:29–30). Because of this, the sufferings of this present age are not worth comparing with the glory to be revealed to us. Indeed, we groan along with all of creation as we await our full adoption and the redemption of our bodies (8:22–23). That's what the "therefore" is there for!

Jesus has fulfilled it all: Law, priesthood, sacrificial system, kingship, and Suffering Servant—all meet in the one God-man Jesus Christ. This is the great theological vision of Paul in the book of Romans. That's what the "therefore" is there for!

## A Closer Look at Romans 12:1–2

Romans 1–11 is the first half of the gospel, stating what God has done for us in Jesus Christ. Romans 12–15 is what God is doing in us to form us and conform us fully to the image of Christ. The word *therefore*, as we noted, marks the seam between Romans 1–11 and Romans 12–15.

The word of God through the apostle Paul entreats us, urges us, and pleads with us for nothing less than a full orientation of our entire being, heart, mind, and body, toward the worship of the living God. This is why worship is a means of grace. It carries us as a worshiping community into the very presence of the triune God, and in His presence we are reoriented to reflect that presence in the world.

These two verses (12:1–2) are actually summary verses that capture the whole ethical and formational life of the Christian. The mercies of God in verse 1 represent in seed form all that I have summarized from Romans 1–11. The whole gospel is nothing less than a testimony to the mercy of God. The word *therefore* points back to the first eleven chapters, and the phrase "mercies of God" summarizes them in three words. What is the gospel? It is the mercy of God. What does the mercy of God look like? Jesus Christ. How is the mercy of God in Jesus Christ made manifest to the world? It is made manifest in and through our lives.

Paul then tells us to "present our bodies" to God. This phrase is in seed form Paul's theology of the body. This is the death knell to the undue separation of our physical bodies from our spiritual lives. God fashioned our bodies at the dawn of the creation as the perfect vessel for His eventual redemptive plan to send His only Son into the world as the embodied Jesus of Nazareth, God in the flesh. Not only do our bodies point to the incarnation (which is in our past), but they also point to the future resurrection (which is still in our future). We are living testimonies to both the first and second coming of Christ into the world.

Paul goes on to tell us to present our bodies as a "living sacrifice." It is hard for us in the twenty-first century to fully appreciate how much sacrifice framed the religious consciousness of the ancient world. Religion was tied to pagan sacrifice. Sacrifice was also integral to the Old Testament vision as the foundation for the doctrine of substitutionary atonement. The people of God once sacrificed bulls, goats, lambs, and rams, but now, Paul says, those are shadows that have been fulfilled by Jesus, the final sacrifice. In response to that, we offer our bodies as a *living sacrifice*. Not a dead sacrifice, but a living one. We are those who have been made alive by the work of Christ, and as the redeemed people of God we offer ourselves, our living selves to God! But it must be a holy sacrifice—a sanctified sacrifice as Paul says, "holy and pleasing to God—this is your true and proper worship."

## Worship as a Means of Grace

When we talk about worship as a means of grace, we must never forget the power of physically gathering together as the people of God for public worship. When we come together, we sing songs of praise and celebrate collectively through words and actions what God has done for us.

During the multiple lockdowns during the COVID-19 pandemic, millions of Christians around the world were unable to physically attend worship services. We should salute the remarkable energy and creativity that took place in churches to deliver worship through various online formats during that time. However, we should never regard public worship in a gathered space as the equivalent of those same people scattered in their homes watching the service online. Why is this? There are several important reasons for this.

First, the public embodiment of God's gathered people is commanded by Scripture. We are called by God to meet together. The Word of God commands us, saying, "Let us consider how to stir up one another to love and good works, not neglecting to meet together as is the habit of some, but encouraging one another, and all the more as you see the Day drawing near" (Heb. 10:24–25). This command of God's Word supersedes any executive order or command from the governing authorities. The Diocletian persecution, sometimes called the Great Persecution, is widely believed to be the most severe persecution ever inflicted against Christians from the hands of the Roman Empire. It took place in the year 303 and was the result of a series of government edicts issued against Christians.

Christians were forbidden to meet together, the clergy were required to make sacrifices to the Roman gods, and all Christians were purged from the army—and those are just a few examples of the challenges Christians faced. If they disobeyed these edicts, Christians had their property seized, they were arrested and beaten, and many were executed by being fed to the lions as a public spectacle. But even during this period, they kept meeting together. They met in secret locations like the catacombs. They used secret signals to indicate safe spaces (this is the origin of the use of IXTHUS). We should never allow any government authority to forbid Christians from meeting together. We may agree to forgo meetings for a short period due to a national crisis, but it is a decision that we must make, rather than one that we allow to be made for us. This is an important principle that will prepare us for the increasingly totalitarian tendencies of modern governments.

Second, public worship in a gathered space is a powerful means of grace. Our bodies serve as a bridge to the grace of God in our lives. Indeed, it is the *physical* body that is able to make visible the *spiritual* realities of God's nature and covenantal love. As we gather together, all the means of grace happen in and through your body. Your body is baptized and takes the Lord's Supper. Your ears hear the Word of God and your lips preach or share the Word of God. Your feet and hands serve the poor and your tongue prays and your heart worships. We lay hands on the sick and they are healed. All the means of grace are made active in and through our bodies because our bodies are designed to image God's purposes and convey His grace. When we meet together, all of these gifts and graces are made manifest.

Third, public worship is the great act of weekly reorientation for the people of God. Living in modern society can be very destabilizing for Christian identity. The wider culture disdains the things of God. The bulk of the advertisement and entertainment industry reinforces values that are antithetical to the Christian faith. We are so immersed in these alternative values we can easily become co-opted by them. Yet, when we gather together for worship in a common space and we see and hear other Christians, it can be a powerfully reorienting experience. It is in public worship that we find ourselves reminded of the nature of God and His purposes in the world. We are reminded of the hope we have in the gospel. We are renewed in our realization that the world is utterly lost without the good news of Jesus Christ. This is one of the great purposes of publicly gathering together as the people of God. This is why Paul goes on to say in verse 2, "Do not be conformed to this world, but be transformed by the renewal of your mind." The word in the Greek translated here as *transformed* is the same word for "metamorphosis." Metamorphosis is the process that changes something into something completely different. This is one of the great realities of what happens as we gather in worship; we are transformed. In Christian theology this means the transformation of us from being sinners to being sanctified. That is a profound metamorphosis!

Fourth, public worship equips us and transforms us to be His ambassadors in the world. Romans 12 gives us the goal of the Christian life. The whole hinge text is centered around the phrase "which is your spiritual worship" (Rom. 12:1). The self-sacrifice of our lives before God and the world is the heart of what it means to be a worshiping community. True worship is the arena through which our lives become conformed to the image of God. This is why we worship Jesus Christ, for the full restoration of the image of God in us is tied directly to Christ being formed in us and the image of God in Christ shining in and through our lives. This is why Paul, in his letter to the Galatians, tells them that he is in anguish over them because they were trying to conform to God's will by turning to the Law. The Law is good, but, in the end, we cannot keep the Law in our own power, and it is only through the grace of God in Christ that His will is manifest through us. Paul says, "I am again in the anguish of child-birth until Christ is formed in you!" (Gal. 4:19). In other words, sanctification happens only as we allow Christ to be formed in us through the power of the Holy Spirit. God has destined us to have our hearts and minds completely renewed, and He has the power to redirect our hearts so that our goal and passion is nothing less than the "pleasing and perfect will" of God (Rom. 12:2 NIV). This is our act of worship. Each week we are renewed afresh in His presence, and we carry that with us throughout the week. D. L. Moody once said that he had heard a preacher say, "The world has scarcely seen what can be done through a man or woman whose heart and life and affections have been completely and wholly turned over and consecrated unto him." Moody said he told the Lord that night, "I aim to be that man."[16] May that be our aim. May our whole lives become an act of spiritual worship.

---

16. Paul Gericke, *Crucial Experiences in the Life of D. L. Moody* (Chicago: Insight Press, 1978).

# Chapter Nine

# The Psalms as a Means of Grace

## SCRIPTURAL BACKGROUND: PSALM 1

Dietrich Bonhoeffer in his timeless book *Psalms: The Prayer Book of the Bible* wrote, "Whenever the Psalter is abandoned, an incomparable treasure vanishes from the Christian church. With its recovery will come unsuspected power."[17] I noted in the last chapter that the great project of the next generation of Christians is the recovery of biblical Christianity in place of the tepid, domesticated version that is currently being taken for the real thing. That recovery project is a massive one, but one of the elements

---

17. Dietrich Bonhoeffer, *Psalms: The Prayer Book of the Bible* (Minneapolis, MN: Augsburg Press, 1975), 26.

of that will be the rediscovery of the Psalms as a means of grace. This purpose of this chapter is to highlight how the Psalms serve as a special means of grace for the church, as this book rings together three of the means of grace into one place: Scripture, worship, and prayer.

God has placed a worship book right in the middle of the Bible. The book of Psalms is the only inspired worship book we have, and it is designed to be foundational for all Christian worship. Hymns and choruses are wonderful, and they go back to the earliest Christians. Yet, the church sang the Psalms as its *primary* hymnbook for most of our history. The Psalms are the singular shared canon of worship for the people of God for all time. It was not until the eighteenth century that hymns began to overtake psalms as the primary way Christians worshiped. By the twentieth century most churches no longer used psalms in worship, except perhaps as a responsive reading.

The Psalms are written not in prose but in Hebrew poetry, and they were given to us to be sung. When we think of poetry, we associate it primarily with some kind of regular meter and rhyme. Hebrew poetry does not function in the same way. Hebrew poetry is based on what is called "thought" rhyming, rather than sound rhyming. This means that rather than having the last syllable end with the same sound as in a classic English poem, a Hebrew poem expresses a thought and then restates that same thought in parallel form, or sometimes by contrasting two ideas. Thus, you have two similar thoughts side by side, creating a kind of thought rhyme. There are many variations on this in the Hebrew, just as there are many variations in English poetry, but this is the basic idea. It is understandably difficult to comprehend how you can open the Psalms and start to sing them. This is true because singing from a known tune (such as a hymn tune you know like "Amazing Grace" or "The Church's One Foundation") doesn't work because psalms in the Bible, as noted, were based on a different understanding of poetry than what we use for congregational singing. But we know that psalms were meant to be sung because dozens of psalms contain specific musical instructions or indications at the top of the psalm. For example, the phrase "for the director of music" is quite common (Psalms 18–22), as is "with stringed instruments" or "flutes" (e.g., Psalms 4–6). Other psalms specify which tune is to be sung (Psalm 22, which is to be sung to the tune "The Doe of the Morning"). The fact that the Psalms are given as a book of worship is part of God's inspiration, and it should not be treated like a book of history or prophecy. It is its own genre, a collection of 150 songs. To put it plainly, the Psalms are meant for singing, so why don't we sing them? The church has responded over the centuries to this challenge by chanting the Psalms or by creating what is known as metrical psalters. A metrical psalter takes each psalm and writes it in a regular meter and time so that it can be easily sung.

As an example, let us take the familiar Psalm 100 and look at how one of the verses is rendered in regular meter.

> Enter his gates with thanksgiving,
> and his courts with praise!
> give thanks to him and praise his name. (v. 4 NIV)

This verse is not in regular meter and therefore it cannot be easily sung. Notice how the first line has eight syllables, the second line has five, and the third line has eight. However, with a few changes, it can be rendered into what is known as "common meter" (8 syllables, 6 syllables, 8 syllables, 6 syllables):

> Enter His gates with thanksgiving,
> Into His courts with praise.
> Give thanks to Him and bless His name,
> His praises sing always.

This verse can now be sung, for example, to the tune of "Amazing Grace." Why don't you try it? In fact, you can sing this verse to any common meter tune. You could sing it to the tune of "O for a Thousand Tongues to Sing" or "O God, Our Help in Ages Past" and so forth. When this process is done with all the psalms, the result is known as a metrical psalter. There have been many of these produced over the years, including the *Scottish Psalter* dating back to 1650. My wife, Julie, and I produced one several years ago, and it is available through Seedbed.[18] This site is a resource providing all 150 psalms in regular meter and rhyme, with a list of hymn tunes for each psalm, including a link to a continuous loop audio of Julie playing on the piano while you sing through the psalm.

Psalm singing is a powerful means of grace. It was not until Julie and I were in our fifties that we began to really discover the power of daily psalm singing. Since 2011, we have been singing psalms every morning and have found it to be a great source of spiritual strength and growth. In this chapter, I want to talk about some of the larger themes of

---

18. Julie and Timothy Tennent, *A Metrical Psalter: The Book of Psalms Set to Meter for Singing* (Franklin, TN: Seedbed Publishing, 2017). See http://psalms.seedbed.com.

the Psalms, which can help us to encounter the Psalms as a means of grace, regardless of whether you sing them or just read them devotionally.

Most Christians today encounter the Psalms by reading them or memorizing a few favorite ones, but we do not often realize the full import of the Psalms as a way to encounter the whole Bible. The book of Psalms is a collecting point for the whole of Scripture since all the great themes of the Old Testament find poetic expression in the Psalms, and they, in turn, point to the great theme of fulfillment in the New Testament. So, whether you read or sing the Psalms, you are implanting the whole of the Bible into your heart. The diversity and richness of the Psalms are also quite astonishing. Let's examine some of them.

## The Psalms as 150 Journeys

The book of Psalms is a collection of five books, divided into 150 different psalms. You should look at the 150 psalms as 150 little spiritual journeys. Some of these 150 journeys can be comforting, but others can be very disruptive and tumultuous. The Psalms hammer away at us as much as they comfort us. They both inspire and shape us. Most of all, they bring us into a far deeper understanding of who God is and what it means to walk before Him in the world. The first psalm sets the basic framework for all the 150 journeys. Psalm 1 establishes what is known as the "two ways": the way of the righteous and the way of the wicked. The Psalms regularly set forth the basic contours of the righteous life and, with equal clarity, the way that leads to sorrow and destruction. Psalm 1, for example, describes the righteous as a person who meditates on God's Word, delights in following the Lord, and flourishes like a palm tree. The wicked, in contrast, resist God's ways and, in the end, will not stand in the day of judgment. This is reinforced in dozens of ways throughout all 150 journeys. It is important to read or sing through the entire psalm and allow it to conform our perspective about life to God's perspective.

## The Scope of Worship in the Psalms

When you take a typical hymnbook and place it side by side with the Psalter, you will find that the two are very different kinds of worship books. First of all, hymns typically fit within a fairly confined frame of space and time, contain perhaps three to five verses, and take approximately three to four minutes to sing. Part of the art of reading or singing the Psalms involves breaking this expectation and just letting the text of the psalm be its own unique journey. Some psalms, like Psalm 117, are very short and can be read or sung in less than a minute, whereas other psalms, like Psalm 78, are much longer. Some psalms are peaceful, others turbulent. Sometimes we have only the voice of the psalmist, whereas in other psalms we experience rapid shifts between God's voice, the psalmist's voice, or even the voice or thoughts of the wicked.

When compared to a hymnbook, the subject scope of the Psalms is also far more diverse. Hymns tend to be acts of praise and adoration, with some exceptions. The Psalms have some of those, but the 150 journeys of the Psalter also contain laments, historical surveys, warnings, penitence, struggles against enemies, deep questioning of God and His purposes, and longing for a future hope, to name a few. It is, indeed, a very different kind of terrain. Sometimes when you encounter a psalm, you have to buckle your seatbelt for the journey because it can be kind of a wild ride!

The 150 set journeys that are given to us in the Psalms are like train tracks. As you sing or read them, you lay those particular tracks down in your heart, which prepares you for the time when you need to have that particular journey in your life. You may wake up one morning and encounter a lament psalm when you are feeling great and do not even remotely feel like lamenting, but that is part of the power of the long-term catechesis of the psalms. You may not be in lament, but someone you know is, and, indeed, the world is always groaning in lament and we need to be reminded of that. The 150 psalms proactively lay 150 life journeys into our lives, and the scope of these journeys is astonishing.

*The psalms of personal struggle brought before God.* The Psalms reveal the depth of God's character in the midst of all kinds of human turmoil. The Psalms draw us not away from the world but boldly into it. Many of them are rooted in the soil of pain, conflict, and disruption. In the midst of those struggles, the psalmist also clings to the sure and certain character of God as revealed in a beautiful set of words that cycle through the Psalms: covenant love, mercy, justice, righteousness, and peace. When we encounter disruptions in life, if untutored by the Psalms, we can have faith crises. But the Psalms call us to lean into our questions, lean into the disruptions, and on the other side, to rediscover the deeper side of the gospel and what it truly means to share in the sufferings of Christ as we walk through the world.

*The history psalms.* These are wonderful treasures and often give us a unique perspective on history. For example,

Psalm 105 and 106 are both history psalms, a genre we never encounter in our hymnody. Psalm 105 tells the history of Israel from *God's perspective*; it is a glorious celebration of His mighty acts in creation, at the Red Sea, at Sinai, and so forth. Psalm 106 tells the same history from the *human perspective* and openly chronicles that history in a way that we would never do in our worship hymns or choruses, recalling our rebellion, our stubbornness of heart, our propensity to resist God's work, and our inclination to idolatry. Those two psalms alone give us a window into the whole of Christian history like few acts of worship ever could.

*Questioning psalms.* The Psalms are filled with hard questions, sometimes coming at us with unrelenting force. This is another rarity in modern acts of worship. For example, Psalm 74 has the boldness to ask questions like: Why have you rejected us? Why does your anger burn against your own sheep? How long will you allow foes to deride your name? Why do you hold your hand back?

We just don't sing songs like that! But the Psalter is the great permission slip to explore our deepest pain in ways that are shocking and unsettling to our normal sentiment about God and what the life of prayer and an act of worship really looks like. Psalm 13 is another psalm that raises questions before God in a way that is quite startling. The psalm opens with a series of stark questions that we don't often associate with prayer: How long will you forget me? How long will you hide your face from me? How long will I have sorrow in my heart all day long? How long will my enemy be exalted over me? It is important that we know that we can put our deepest questions before God.

*Warning psalms.* Another class of psalms are those that give some kind of warning to the people of God. Psalm 95 is a great example of this. The modern church often just reads the first seven verses that contain some of the most joyous calls to worship in the Scriptures: "O come, let us sing to the LORD . . . Let us come into his presence with thanksgiving . . . O come, let us worship and bow down . . . for he is our God, and we are the people of his pasture." Yet, the psalm ends with a strong admonition and warning to not "harden our hearts" or "put him to the test." We are admonished to not "go astray" in our hearts. The Psalms are designed to be both our praise and worship to God as well as His instruction and admonition to us.

*Penitential psalms.* One of the most important classes of psalms is known as the Penitential Psalms. While dozens of psalms reflect words of repentance and remorse over sin (both individual and corporate), church tradition dating back to the fifth century set aside seven of the psalms as Penitential Psalms (Psalms 6, 32, 38, 51, 102, 130, and 143). They draw us into a journey of repentance and reflection on the power and presence of sin in our lives, in the people of God, in those who oppose the people of God, and in the world in general. The Penitential Psalms do not focus merely on the sin that is within us but also on the sin and transience that is out there in the world.

*Lament psalms.* There are many psalms dedicated to lament. Some of these psalms are expressions of personal lament because of specific dire circumstances facing the psalmist (e.g., Psalms 22 and 88). Others are expressions of corporate lament because of the general state of the nation as a whole (e.g., Psalms 74 and 79). Still others are laments about God's silence and seeming absence. Typically, these lament psalms are addressed to God and directly tell God the nature of the lament. The psalmist is free to suggest solutions to God as to how it might be resolved, but the laments are actually strong expressions of trust in God, because lament is the voice of faith, not despair. The sheer act of lamenting to God means that the psalmist trusts that God is there and that God hears and cares. There are many other classes of psalms, but this gives some examples to highlight the remarkable scope of the Psalms. The Psalms represent a kind of curriculum for life as they cover such a wide variety of human experience before God.

## The Psalms as a Window to Jesus Christ

Christians naturally read or sing the Psalms through the lens of the New Testament and the fulfillment celebrated there. In this respect, certain psalms have entered the life of the church with tremendous force because they are directly applied to Jesus. For example, one's mind quickly goes to Psalm 110, especially the phrase "you are priest forever after the order of Melchizedek" (v. 4), which is quoted five times in the New Testament. Perhaps we might think of Psalm 2, one of the great messianic psalms quoted in Acts, twice in Hebrews, and three times in Revelation: "You are my Son; today I have begotten you," which is both Hebrew poetry and New Testament proclamation. And, certainly, one thinks of Psalm 118, which has the distinction of being the most-quoted psalm in the New Testament, particularly the phrases "the stone that the builders rejected has become the cornerstone" (v. 22) and "blessed is he who comes in the name of the LORD!" (v. 26). Psalm 22, likewise, was explicitly heard on the lips of Jesus as He hung on the cross, applying to Himself that haunting question, "My God, my

God, why have you forsaken me?" (v. 1). However, other psalms like Psalm 80 and 132 point to Jesus even though they are never quoted in the New Testament. Psalm 80 provides five of the richest images of Christ that are now part of our Christology: Christ as Shepherd, Christ as the True Vine, Christ as God's Son, Christ as the Son of Man, and Christ who sits at God's right hand.

However, the 150 psalms do more than merely *point* to Christ. We must remember that the Psalms were the only prayer book or worship book Jesus ever knew. He, too, sang them every day, and He still walks with His people through the Psalms in a way that is hard to describe if you have not experienced it. Christ is the voice behind all the psalms. He laments with us, carries our sorrows, embodies Israel's history, warns us, and stands with us against the array of those who stand opposed to God's rule and reign. He embodies all of the eschatological hope in the Psalms. He is God's Word of comfort and grace to us, and He stands in the midst of all the psalms, not merely as the fulfillment of them but as one who sings and cries out to God with us. We never sing these psalms alone. When we sing Psalm 88 about the darkness, Jesus is singing with us because He, too, sang it that night in Caiaphas's pit. When we sing Psalm 82, Jesus is also angry at the injustices of unjust judges. When we sing Psalm 70, Jesus is also crying out, "Make haste, O God, to deliver me! O LORD, make haste to help me" (v. 1).

This is also what finally helps us when we encounter the Psalms of Imprecation that call down curses on our enemies. It must be remembered that these troubling verses are not about us acting out these imprecations but asking *God* to act to right wrongs in the world. Even though Christ teaches us to love our enemies, we continue to recognize that the demonic principalities and powers are arrayed against us, and these psalms can be directed toward those forces. More importantly, Jesus Christ Himself bears these curses through His death on the cross. Praying openly to God about our own pain and struggles with others not only helps us to put these deep matters into God's hands but also stands as a reminder that Jesus ultimately bears our pain on the cross.

This chapter contains only a quick overview of the Psalms. However, I hope that even this short meditation will begin to open many new doors for us as we see how uniquely positioned the Psalms are to guide us, help us, and give voice to many of our deepest prayers. The Psalms are truly a means of grace for us.

# Chapter Ten

# Love as the Supreme Means of Grace

*By Joe Dongell*

*Author's note: At Asbury we are privileged to have many godly and wise professors who teach and train our students. Dr. Joseph Dongell serves as our professor of biblical studies. He has made a special study of love as a means of grace. Therefore, I thought it would only be fitting to ask Joe Dongell to complete this book by writing the final chapter on love as a means of grace.*

The purpose of this chapter is to bring the ship into port and draw to a close this voyage examining the means of grace. This final chapter will focus on two areas: 1) to emphasize key points about the means of grace in general and 2) to bring us to the destination of our journey, the pier that we shall simply call *love*. Somehow, our journey must end there, if indeed, "God is love," just as Scripture declares (1 John 4:8, 16).

So first, let's double-check our trajectory through the means of grace, since it is all too easy for us to lose our bearings even on this last stage of the voyage. We must be clear about the means of grace, since many of us have found them to be a problem, a hindrance, or a cause of confusion, perhaps even giving birth to pride on the one hand or despair on the other.

Let's divide the expression into its two parts—"the means" and "grace"—and begin with the second element. To speak of *grace* is to grasp one of the Bible's central themes: that God is a *gracious* God. Put differently, God is a *giving* God.

Now, as Creator, surely God has been a giver all along. God has been giving to us creatures our life, breath, hope, joy, purpose in living, family, friends, livelihoods, pleasures, food, laughter, and a thousand other delights of beauty and goodness. However bleak human life can be (and often is) and however sinful we have become (and often are), God has been continually pouring fabulous gifts out upon all creatures. I love the majestic KJV translation of Psalm 145:15–16: "The eyes of all wait upon thee; and thou givest them their meat in due season. Thou openest thine hand, and satisfiest the desire of every living thing."

Even more, as Redeemer, God has richly poured out upon all who repent and believe even more grace in the form of a thousand richer blessings: forgiveness, peace, the stirrings of eternal life, adoption into God's family, healing for body and soul, ministry callings, ministry gifts, ministry fruitfulness, joy in serving people in the name of Jesus, joy in belonging to the people of God, joy in seeing true success in our work, hope in the midst of pain and loneliness, and on and on.

To put it another way, whenever we speak of the means of *grace*, we are boldly subscribing to the conviction that God is the supreme *giver* and that we ourselves are eternally and irreversibly dependent creatures. We are *receivers* by nature, and we always will be. When we get this sorted out, most everything else falls into place. As James put it, "Every good endowment and every perfect gift is from above, coming down from the Father of lights with whom there is no variation or shadow due to change" (1:17 RSV). Or as Paul insisted when chiding Corinthian pride, "What do you have that you did not receive?" (1 Cor. 4:7). God gives; we receive. We live and thrive, whether physically or spiritually, by divine gift-giving, by divine *grace*.

But as we grow in grace, and as our spiritual eyes open wider to see truth more clearly, we will become painfully aware of our deficits, our fears, our sins, our weaknesses, our ineffectiveness, our blindness, our confusions. . . . We become ever more alert to how desperately we need God to pour out specific blessings, specific divine gifts to address this or that specific challenge staring us in the face right now.

So how do we get God to give us what we so desperately need? Are there any *means* by which we can trigger God to send a heavier rain of *grace* on this or that plot of dry ground in our lives? Put this way, the question probably sounds perverse to many of us. We will likely protest, "No, of course we can't make God do things. We can't pull a trigger to activate God's giving. God will do whatever God wants, however God wants, whenever God wants. That's what it means to be God! Any other view is pure blasphemy!"

Blasphemy, indeed, unless the Bible tells a different story! And we do find that all the way through the Bible, God Himself actually sets up all sorts of contracts in the form of "If you do this, I will do that." Strange, that the

Sovereign God would tie His activity in any way to ours! But it's everywhere across the Old Testament and right into the New Testament, especially in the teaching of Jesus. Of course, Jesus was free to act unilaterally and unconditionally. He could, and did, just walk up and heal someone or exorcise demons without asking for any human cooperation. But just as commonly, Jesus asked people to *do something* as an implied condition for Jesus to intervene: "Fill those jars with water!" (and I will do something amazing for this embarrassed wedding party); "Move that stone!" (and I will do something amazing for you grieving sisters); "Stretch out your hand!" (and I will do something amazing to reverse your paralysis); or "Eat my flesh and drink my blood, and I will infuse my life into you!"

So how is this different from pure paganism, from the idea that we human beings can control divine powers and get God to do things for us? It is essential to recognize two distinctions.

First, in the Bible's view of these divine contracts, it is God Himself who has specified the actions He wants us to do. God has named the very triggers that will move God's heart and hand to act on our behalf. Quite unlike the experimental approach of paganism that tries out this trick and then that one, we approach God in the very pathways that God has actually revealed to us. So, in approaching God in these very ways that God has appointed (ordained, instituted, mapped out, revealed, *given* to us), we are *humbly accepting God's own guidance*. We are *obeying* God's commands and *trusting* that God will indeed fulfill His promise to respond to us as we walk and wait in these pathways. See the pattern? "Do these things *that I have specified* (the means)," says the Lord, "And I will do for you amazing things (grace)," in God's time and way, of course.

The second distinction is this: the Bible makes it clear that our actions themselves, these means, these divinely instituted pathways (whether we have in mind prayer, or fasting, or studying the Scripture, or receiving the Lord's Supper, or gathering together in Jesus' name, and so on), these actions *have absolutely no power or merit in themselves*. Mr. Wesley compared them (in his sermon "The Means of Grace") to "dry leaves." Yes, grip them in your hands and they turn to dust! And so while paganism is always enamored by ritual actions themselves, mesmerized by their supposed power, we know that our practices and disciplines have *no power at all* in themselves. We continually put our whole trust in God alone and in God's scripturally published promises to meet us as we walk in these means that God Himself has provided.

Remember the story of Naaman the Syrian leper (2 Kings 5)? The prophet Elisha gave him instructions for doing what would trigger God's healing power: "Go and wash in the Jordan, seven times" (v. 10). Naaman would never have proposed such a thing and had other ideas about how to affect his own cure. How odd! How counterintuitive! How revolting to a man of his stature! But, finally, he humbled his heart and obediently did what God had commanded, trusting that God would fulfill His promise to meet his need.

How wonderful it is, then, that we are not left to wonder, or guess, or grope about in trial and error with only a faint hope of receiving divine help and blessing! God has not said, "Seek me in darkness" (cf. Isa. 45:19) but "This is the way, walk in it!" (Isa. 30:21). So we live in great confidence, knowing that "God, who never lies" (Titus 1:2) has sworn to meet and bless us as we walk toward Him in the means of grace that He Himself has *given* to us.

But now let's focus on the matter of *grace* itself and its actual content. Up to this point I have been sharing about God's gracious blessings in the *plural*, because God does give us *many* things, and many different *sorts* of things. This is what all good fathers love to do. But as we mature spiritually, we will discover that, above and beyond all the blessings and benefits God gives, one supreme gift rises above everything: God's gift of *Himself*, God's very presence realized and known in our lives. We remember that to the ancient tribe of Levi God said, "No, I'm not going to give you land, however wonderful and valuable that might be: I'm giving you Myself! I am your inheritance" (cf. Num. 18:20). Likewise, Moses knew that God's *very presence* was the real prize. Though God had offered an angel to accompany Israel into the promised land to guarantee their safety and prosperity, Moses turned down that attractive offer for something far better: "Unless *you* go with us, we *will not go up* into the land" (cf. Ex. 33:15). Wesley makes the same point (in the sermon I've already referenced, "The Means of Grace") when giving final advice about practicing the means: "Seek *God alone*. Nothing short of *God* can satisfy your soul" (emphasis added).

But as the story of Scripture unfolds, we learn that God has had an inner craving all along to give to humanity something God cherishes above all else. (Note that this is the instinct all real lovers have: we want to give to our beloved what is most precious to us.) And so we discover that, at the appointed time, God gave to the world His own greatest treasure: the Eternal Son who had been resting in the Father's bosom from all eternity (John 1:1, 18). As we seek God alone, we will discover that fellowship with the Father leads us into a focused fellowship with the Son, the one in whom all the fullness of God dwells (Col. 1:19)!

This grand story moves ahead still further! As we continue seeking God alone, we will learn that the Father and Son have conspired to give an even more refined, precious, and intimate gift to all fervent seekers: the gift of the Holy Spirit. The Spirit is no impersonal power, no strange ghost, but the third person of the Holy Trinity, who, perhaps as Augustine suggested, is the very bond of love between the Father and the Son, so that their combined gift would become the Master Distributor of all divine gifts and blessings.

But is there another step in the gift-giving? If we keep seeking God alone, might we discover that the Spirit now has a gift to give, a gem of unspeakable value that captures like nothing else the very essence and character of the triune God? I think that John Wesley, in his careful and synthetic reading of the Scripture, has repeatedly and emphatically answered this question with a resounding yes and has named that gift as nothing other than love. As he urges in one passage in his *Plain Account of Christian Perfection*:

*Love is the highest gift of God*; humble, gentle, patient love; that all visions, revelations, [or] manifestations whatever, are little things compared to love; and that all [other] gifts . . . are either the same with or infinitely inferior to [love]. [Therefore, you] should be thoroughly [aware] of this—*the heaven of heavens is love. There is nothing higher in religion; there is, in effect, nothing else*; if you look for *anything but more love*, you are looking wide of the mark, you are getting out of the royal way. And when you are asking others, "Have you received this or that blessing?" if you mean anything but more love, you mean wrong; you are leading them out of the way, and putting them [on] a false scent. Settle it then in your heart, that from the moment God has saved you from all sin, you are to *aim at nothing more but more of that love* described in the thirteenth [chapter] of [First] Corinthians. *You can go no higher than this*, till you are carried into Abraham's bosom.[19]

There are good, scriptural reasons for seeking love above all:

---

19. John Wesley, *Plain Account of Christian Perfection*, Section 25, Question 33, emphasis added.

1. In seeking love, we are seeking God's *very essence*, for as we read in 1 John, God is love (4:8, 16). As Wesley put it, "[Love] *is* [God's] *darling, his reigning attribute* [shedding] *an amiable glory on all his other perfections.*"[20] So think of it! To be filled with God's gift of love is to become like God in the highest sense possible for us mortals, whether in time or across all eternity!

2. In seeking love, we are seeking what will govern and enliven all other gifts. From 1 Corinthians 13 we learn that if love does not fill our hearts, then all the spiritual gifts, all the gifts of ministry, will stagger and slump in weakness (at best) or (at worst) will putrefy into a slimy mass of selfish, toxic fumes. But by implication, when love does fill our hearts, our gifts are purified and aligned for genuine service, energized to accomplish the mighty "labor of love" (1 Thess. 1:3) in effective, life-giving service.

3. In seeking love, we are seeking the fountain of all other virtues, the fountain of all holiness. Wesley understood, as have many exegetes and saints throughout history,

---

20. See John Wesley's commentary on 1 John 4:8 in his *Explanatory Notes Upon the New Testament* (New York: Lane & Tippett, 1847), 637, emphasis added.

that the fruit of the Spirit described in Galatians 5 is not a cluster of nine individual fruits, as if each were a separate agendum to be pursued. No. The fruit of the Spirit is *love*, and all the following virtues are merely describing the natural rivulets flowing out of love. If my heart is filled with love, then I shall be kind, and good, and patient, and so on. Since the infilling of love displaces all that is unlike itself, specifically the flesh and all of its works, then the infusion of love creates a holy heart. As Wesley put it, "Love is the sum of Christian sanctification; it is the one kind of holiness [there is]."[21]

So let me summarize to this point: I have described the *means* of grace as those practices, habits, rites, and disciplines that God Himself has given to us, clearly marking out a pathway for us to follow, through which (when we walk in them in obedience and trust) God has promised to give us grace; that is, all manner of divine gifts. Then I have laid out a more refined accounting of those gifts, of *grace* culminating in the gift of God's very self (Father, Son, and Spirit), who then together long to fill us with their choicest gift: love. All the means of grace, therefore, when

---

21. See Wesley's sermon "On Patience."

they are practiced in purity and aimed at their loftiest goal, are aimed at love. Seek to be filled with love, above all else! This kind of biblical love should not be confused in any way with the way the word *love* is bandied about in our contemporary culture, projected in films, or displayed on billboards or advertisements. This is not the sentimental, often self-orienting, love of popular discourse and romance novels. Love in the Scriptures refers to God's covenantal commitment to "will our good." This is a costly, self-donating, self-sacrificing love, not rooted in any passing emotive feeling but arising out of God's covenantal commitment to each and every one of us. For us to be filled with love is to be filled with a God-like commitment to will the good of the other, even if it costs us everything.

But what realistic hope is there for being filled with this kind of divine love? None! I'll say it again: there is no realistic hope of ever experiencing such a filling! Why? Because it's not realistic. By realistic, I have in mind whatever most of us would judge to be normal, typical, reasonable according to the wisdom of most sane and rational people, believed by most people to be within our capacity to obtain. In other words, typical or average. Yet, there is hope for such a filling! In Ephesians 3:14–19, Paul offers a prayer for us that is very powerful. Here we find

Paul, in all of his apostolic wisdom and authority, dropping to his knees and asking the Father to give the very highest divine gift to his readers who (it is important to note) were already believers, already "in Christ," already "seated in heavenly places," already "raised to new life" through their fusion with the resurrected Christ. What will he ask for these well-established believers?

First, he asks that they be inwardly strengthened (3:16) and that Christ would dwell somehow even more deeply and permanently in their hearts than he already does (3:17a). But then the prayer ascends even more sharply toward its pinnacle as Paul asks that they may be able to comprehend the incomprehensible dimensions of the love of Christ (3:18), which in turn brings the apostle to this most glorious prize at the absolute apex: to be filled with all the fullness of God (3:19). Think of it! To be filled with all the fullness of God! Put differently, to be filled with that which fills God. But what is that?

There is not sufficient space in this chapter to lay out a lengthy argument, but I find myself convinced by those who have concluded that what fills God can be nothing other than love. Love fills God, and it seems to radiate infinitely in all directions (3:18). And Paul dares to pray that this unbounded divine love would absolutely, completely, and decisively fill all his readers, no doubt in a way that would eclipse their initial infusion with God's love at justification (Rom. 5:5), as well as any other such filling along the way. Astounding!

Paul must be aware that this prayer pushes the limits of propriety, borders on the impossible, and tempts us to back away from its height, catch our breath, and settle for something . . . more realistic . . . more normal . . . more acceptable . . . more reasonable. But the apostle will not back down, and he will not moderate his request. So he caps off his prayer with a solemn doxology to strengthen our resolve in our asking for this impossible filling: "Now to him who is able to do *far more abundantly than all we ask or think*, according to the power at work within us, to him be glory in the church and in Christ Jesus throughout all generations, forever and ever. Amen" (3:20–21, emphasis added). The doxology says it all: for believers to become utterly filled with God's love will require nothing short of the full exercise of God's infinite power (3:20), but . . . should this come about . . . God's glory will glow all the more brightly for all to see (3:21).

As we diligently practice the means of grace, let us not forget God. And as we seek God alone, by walking faithfully and obediently in the well-marked pathways, let us long for the infusion of divine love, God's highest gift (1 Cor. 13:13; 14:1). Then we will discover that the pier of love on which we have landed is not a terminus, the end of our journey, but the beginning of a new venture, governed and energized by love, upon a whole new continent where our hearts will be pure, our service effective, and the aroma emanating from us will be the aroma of God's very presence.

◆ Appendix ◆

# "Means of Grace"
# by Charles Wesley

It has been the tradition over the last twelve years to include a hymn at the end of these devotional books as a way of capturing in worship many of the key themes. This has always been regarded as one of the geniuses of the Wesleyan revivals. We don't just believe doctrine in our heads; we sing it into our hearts! Charles Wesley was so moved by the sermons his brother John preached on the means of grace that he wrote a hymn to capture many of those truths. So, I am including it here as a worshipful summary of our study. Wesley wrote it in common meter (8.6.8.6), so it can be sung to the tune of many familiar hymns, such as "Amazing Grace," "O for a Thousand Tongues to Sing," or even "O God, Our Help in Ages Past." What I love about this hymn is that it never presents the means of grace as anything other than the work of Jesus Christ in and through our lives. As I stated in the first chapter, Jesus Christ is the fountainhead of all the means of grace. The hymn never turns the means into works, as it concludes with the strong testimony to the Reformation doctrine that we are saved by grace. Yet, the whole hymn reverberates with the grand Wesleyan truth that God intends to transform us into His likeness and make us sharers in His holiness.

1. Long have I seem'd to serve Thee, Lord,
   With unavailing pain;
   Fasted, and pray'd and read Thy Word,
   And heard it preach'd, in vain.

2. Oft did I with th'assembly join,
   And near Thine altar drew;
   A form of godliness was mine,
   The power I never knew.

3. To please Thee thus (at last I see)
   In vain I hoped and strove:
   For what are outward things to Thee,
   Unless they spring from love?

4. I see the perfect law requires
   Truth in the inward parts,
   Our full consent, our whole desires,
   Our undivided hearts.

5. But I of *means* have made my boast,
   Of *means* an idol made;
   The spirit in the letter lost,
   The substance in the shade.

6. I rested in the outward law,
   Nor knew its deep design;
   The length and breadth I never saw,
   The height of love Divine.

7. Where am I now, or what my hope?
   What can my weakness do?
   JESUS, to Thee my soul looks up,
   'Tis Thou must make it new.

8. Thine is the work, and Thine alone—
   But shall I idly stand?
   Shall I the written Rule disown,
   And slight my God's command?

9. Wildly shall I from Thine turn back,
   A better path to find;
   Thy holy ordinance forsake,
   And cast Thy words behind?

10. Forbid it, gracious Lord, that I
    Should ever learn Thee so!
    No—let *me* with Thy word comply,
    If I thy love would know.

11. Suffice for me, that Thou, my Lord,
    Hast bid me fast and pray:
    Thy will be done, Thy name adored;
    'Tis only mine t'obey.

12. Thou bidd'st me search the Sacred Leaves,
    And taste the hallow'd Bread:
    The kind commands my soul receives,
    And longs on Thee to feed.

13. Still for Thy loving-kindness, Lord,
    I in Thy temple wait;
    I look to find Thee in Thy Word,
    Or at Thy table meet.

14. Here, *in Thine own appointed ways,*
    I wait to learn Thy will:
    Silent I stand before Thy face,
    And hear Thee say, "Be still!"

15. "Be still—and know that I am God!"
    'Tis all I live to know;
    To feel the virtue of Thy blood,
    And spread its praise below.

16. I wait my vigor to renew,
    Thine image to retrieve,
    The veil of outward things pass through,
    And gasp in Thee to live.

17. I work, and own the labor vain;
    And *thus* from works I cease:
    I strive, and see my fruitless pain,
    Till God create my peace.

18. Fruitless, till Thou Thyself impart,
    Must all my efforts prove:
    They cannot change a sinful heart,
    They cannot purchase love.

19. I do the Thing Thy laws enjoin,
    And *then* the strife gives o'er:
    To Thee I *then* the whole resign:
    I *trust* in means no more.

20. I trust in Him who stands between
    The Father's wrath and me:
    JESUS! Thou great eternal Mean,
    I look for all from Thee.

21. Thy mercy pleads, Thy truth requires,
    Thy promise calls Thee down!
    Not for the sake of my desires—
    But, O! regard Thine own!

22. I seek no motive out of Thee:
    Thine own desires fulfill;
    If now Thy bowels yearn on me,
    On me perform Thy will.

23. Doom, if Thou canst, to endless pains,
    And drive me from Thy face:
    But if Thy stronger love constrains,
    Let me be *saved by grace.*